T0131486

BOTTOMS UP!

MEMOIRS: FORTY-TWO YEARS AS A
SPORT AND COMMERCIAL DIVER

JAMES (JIM) McCUAIG

authorHOUSE

AuthorHouse™
1663 Liberty Drive
Bloomington, IN 47403
www.authorhouse.com
Phone: 1 (800) 839-8640

Published by AuthorHouse   04/16/2020

ISBN: 978-1-7283-5897-0 (sc)
ISBN: 978-1-7283-5898-7 (hc)
ISBN: 978-1-7283-5896-3 (e)

Library of Congress Control Number: 2020906957

Print information available on the last page.

Preface

~~~~~~

FROM THE LAKES and rivers of North Idaho to the oceans, seas and jungle river, it has been quite a trip.

Born in Coeur d'Alene, Idaho, I was naturally attracted to the lake of the same name and the surrounding waters of Hayden Lake, Fernan Lake and the Spokane River.

Swimming, fishing, and water-skiing with friends like Vern Eaton and Russ Parsons were my favorite pastimes. We spent hours playing in the water. Looking for empty bottles was fun on land, and even more exciting beneath the water. In those days, a kid would receive five cents for a pop bottle and three cents for a beer bottle. The cost to see a movie was twenty-five cents, and so it didn't take us long to earn the price of admission.

I attended school in Coeur d'Alene and graduated high school in 1950. I received a diploma from North Idaho Junior College, now known as North Idaho College. I went on to attend Gonzaga University.

Upon receiving a B.A., I joined the staff of Coeur d'Alene Junior High. What a thrill it would be. I taught there two years with my mother, Helen McCuaig, the greatest teacher ever. My dad, Norm McCuaig, who had been the only bus driver in the Coeur d'Alene school district for many years, had been killed in a car accident several years earlier. I regretted the three of us did not get to work together.

With five years of college and a yearly salary of thirty-two hundred dollars, I thought it was time to move to a more lucrative area. I was hired by the Buckley Washington School District with a salary of four thousand dollars. Wow! I was headed up the pay scale.

After several years of teaching in Buckley, and serving as Director of Special Education in Mt. Vernon, Washington, I was hired by the Kent School District, where I remained for the next fourteen years. It was here I became reacquainted with Joe Morris, a fellow Coeur d'Alene Junior High teacher. Joe had accepted a position as a biology teacher at Bellevue High School.

Our mutual love for teaching, science and the sea brought us together and into the world of scuba. We collected marine specimens for the classroom and were amongst the leaders in taking our classrooms to the sea. We taught marine biology and oceanography. While on the beaches, we provided divers to bring up specimens not found in tide pools.

Joe and I became aware we really needed to get into deeper water to experience this new world and find more specimens for our classrooms. Our attempts at scuba diving were ill conceived, scary, and, at times, darn right dangerous. We finally realized our folly and enrolled in a NAUI (National Association of Underwater Instructors) SCUBA (Self Contained Underwater Breathing Apparatus) class.

Upon completing the course, we and many of our diving companions became life-long friends. We became very close with Fred Laister, our mentor, and his family. I spent many happy hours below and above the water with Fred.

After forty-two years in teaching, with the last five years as program manager and instructor at Whatcom Community College, it was time to retire. I had taught at the elementary and secondary level, worked as a school administrator and was a visiting lecturer at Gonzaga University.

I began diving in 1960, dunking my head under the waters of Florida, the Caribbean, California, Washington, Canada, Idaho and Mexico. These places had been my sanctuaries. In 2002, I had my last dive, floating a boathouse in Lake Chatcolet.

Upon retiring, my wife Beverly (a NAUI certified diver) and I moved back to North Idaho, where we continue to make our home.

This book chronicles some of my underwater adventures and chronicles the ups and downs of diving (pun intended).

All the events and stories are real. To all my friends and fellow divers, keep wet.

Chapter 1

The Adventure Begins

UPON JOE MORRIS' arrival in the Seattle area, an old friendship was renewed and the beginning of a new hobby was about to start.

Joe taught biology at Bellevue High School and I taught science and math at Covington Elementary School in Kent, Washington. The year was 1960.

When tides were low, we spent weekends combing through tide pools, digging in the mud and looking for new plants and animals to introduce to our students. Our classrooms were full of bottled sea creatures. The smell of formaldehyde was everywhere, but the strong acrid smell preserved our marine specimens.

It was Joe who introduced me to scuba equipment. You did not need a diving certification to purchase equipment or to buy air for your tanks. We purchased gear from Sears, bought outdated tanks, and shopped garage sales for equipment. It took us several months to pull our equipment together.

Our first adventure was at Alkai Point in West Seattle. We explored without enough weight to keep us down, and then too much weight so we couldn't reach the surface. At one point, we walked to shore underwater. After much trial and error, we began to hug the bottom and fill our goody bags full of specimens. Wow! This was going to be a blast.

We were smart enough not to dive too deep or so we thought. Naive, we did not know the first thirty-three feet of depth is one of the most deadly.

One day, I found a shallow reef loaded with plants and animals. As soon as Joe and I reached the bottom, Joe took off in one direction and I in another. I could see the sun's rays being reflected off the surface. I wasn't too deep. It was warm and the visibility was excellent. I followed the reef until my air was almost gone. On reaching the surface, I was shocked to learn I was a long way from shore. I learned a lesson I'll never forget. Reefs don't always go parallel to the shoreline. The tide was starting to turn. I soon would be swept out to sea gradually. I swam as hard as I could for what seemed like ages. Beginning to cramp, I put my feet down. My fins touched the sand. Walking backward, I made it to safety.

After a few more scary experiences, Joe and I agreed that we needed to take classes in scuba. Death by drowning had no appeal for either of us!

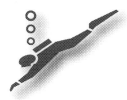

Chapter 2

Scuba Training

ENTERING SKIN DIVER'S Cove in Bellevue, Washington I felt conflicted. I really wanted to take skin diving lessons, but I felt nervous about my lack of swimming skills. My buoyancy (float) level was two feet under the surface, a little deep for breathing. My swimming ability was not all that good. I dreaded the thought of flunking out of a class I so badly wanted to take.

The first night would be spent entirely in the pool. It was our qualification test for the course. Twelve people, of varied ages and sex, would spend four hours in the Olympic-sized pool.

After meeting our teacher, Bob Stanton, and our classmates, we dressed down to our swimsuits and entered the pool area.

Our first challenge was a half-mile swim. We were not allowed to touch the bottom or the sides of the pool. We could, however, use any stroke or combination of strokes, and rest whenever we wanted. I believe I swam the whole way using a side stroke. Well, at least I passed that portion of the test.

The underwater swim was a piece of cake. I swam one length easily and completed about half of the remaining length by pulling myself across the bottom. We weren't penalized for swimming both lengths of the pool. With two tests done, I was feeling pretty good about heading into the evening portion of the class.

The teachers began by asking us to assemble at the north side of the pool. We were asked our weights. They took ten percent of each figure and added that amount of lead to a weight belt. They placed the belt around our middles and showed us how to open the clasp. Our task was to swim across the pool, staying on the surface. I made it halfway across, which was further than others. One elderly man, who must have been in his fifties, was the only one who made it without sinking to the bottom. Those of us who sank unfastened the snap, and popped to the surface. No one panicked so we all passed.

We were ready for our last test and I thought it would be the most difficult. We had to tread water and float for ten minutes. To make matters worse, we would have to have both our hands out of water for the last three minutes. My lungs felt as if they would burst, and my arms and legs were aching. I prayed that I would not cramp up. I didn't think I would make it.

I must have ingested a quart of pool water. Down I went! Kicking hard, I surfaced only to go down again. After what seemed like eons, the final whistle blew. I quickly sprinted to the side of the pool and pulled myself onto the wet cement. I lay panting, but with a smile on my face. I had passed. Everyone had passed.

Joe and I attended classes and pool sessions once a week for six weeks. We would spend two to three hours in class and the same amount of time in the pool.

Our second and third pool sessions were devoted to the use of fins, mask, and snorkel. Each night we started with our quarter-mile swim. What a difference those fins made. It was as if we were flying around the pool. Our leg strength improved with each class. We learned to clear our face masks underwater and clear the snorkel, which always filled with water when we would dive to the bottom. Those next two days were spent doing a lot of diving to the bottom and swimming under and through objects, such as hula hoops. We had to "buddy up" with a different person the entire program. This was a valuable experience as we would have different partners in future years of diving.

Our last three days of pool classes were the most fun. Finally, we were going to use scuba equipment. We were to use all the gear except for the wetsuits (too hot). The equipment included: weight belts and weights, backpacks and tanks, a regulator, and our fins, face plates, and snorkels. Our first regulators were the old two-hose regulators; one hose brought air to us, and one hose was for the expulsion of bad air that we had exhaled.

There were certain advantages and disadvantages of the two-hose regulator. With the two hoses, it was much easier to share air with another, and if the diver lay on one side, the air would be forced into his mouth. A diver's bubbles came out behind him so he didn't have to worry about the bubbles getting under the mask or into the helmet of his wet suit. They also doubled the chances of getting hooked on objects

flag with a white stripe that ran from the top of the mast to the bottom right corner of the flag). The flags would warn all boaters there were divers down and not to approach the area. We also noticed a large boat beyond the flags, slowly trolling back and forth. There were divers on the boat, and they had their binoculars ready and aimed in our direction. One small rubber raft, without a motor, was floating inside the flags near some pilings. The pilings were the remains of an old ferry landing on the very point of Alki. Those manning the rubber raft and the boat off shore, we noticed, were the extra instructors who had given us such a bad time on Panic Night. They were there now to save our bacon if we ran into trouble.

It took time before we were all able to get into the water. Each new diver had to wait for one of our original instructors to take us to the dive site. The owner of Skin Diver's Cove, Mel, became my buddy for my final test. There would be no funny business today. Mel and I completed examining each other's equipment, and then together we shuffled backward into the sound. Walking backwards kept us from tripping over our large fins and taking a nosedive into the sand.

Swimming out to the pilings, Mel gave a signal, and we descended down one of the pilings to the sea floor. Mel pointed to his depth gauge, and I looked at mine. We were at thirty-seven feet. The water was calm and clear. The visibility was excellent and we could see one hundred feet in all directions. I could see our bubbles, small to begin with, then as they reached the surface getting larger and larger until they burst.

I was prepared for what Mel did next. Gently, but firmly, he pushed me back against the piling. My knees were in the sand. I kneeled there silently looking into my buddy's eyes. He motioned for me to clear my face mask. The cold ocean water rushed under the face plate, up around my nose, and into my eyes. I could see little and the temperature of the salt water made me take in a quick breath. Thank heavens no water rushed up my nose.

I quickly put my face mask on, and turned my head to the side. While holding the upward part of the mask, I blew through my nose. Ah ha! Just like in the pool, the water rushed out of the mask and I could see and breathe normal again. Mel gave me an okay signal and let me rest for a few seconds. The next four or five minutes we shared my air. I would take a deep drink of the fresh air and pass my regulator to him. He would breathe on my air for six or seven seconds and then return the regulator to me. Once the task was accomplished, Mel pointed out to sea.

We swam side-by-side farther into the depths. Mel would often stop and point out a sea creature or hand me a sea cucumber to touch. He also pointed out a concealed sole. It was lying on the bottom beneath a shallow covering of sand, just his little eyes popping out.

Ten minutes later, he motioned to me to stop and pointed to his depth gauge. We were now in sixty feet of water. He gave me a pat on the back and motioned toward the beach. We had a leisurely swim back. Reaching a depth of four feet, we stood up and walked backwards to shore.

Mel took a very short breather and grabbed another neophyte. He and the other instructors would use the same routine on all my classmates. As for me, I quickly took off all my gear and wetsuit. After drying myself off, I drank a cup of very hot coffee. Those who completed their swims ate sandwiches, sunbathed, or just visited about the experience. We were all elated. Finally, everyone had finished. We formed a circle around our instructor, Bob, and with a handshake, he gave each of us our cherished NAUI card. It was 1962, which was two years after Joe and I had begun our initial quest into scuba diving. What a day!

I left the classroom portion of the NAUI program for last because of its importance to me in the chapters to follow. Let me start at the beginning.

Though not as exciting as the pool sessions, the classroom lessons were very interesting just the same. It is very important to take classes that teach you more than how to be a proficient swimmer. Learning about the marine plants and animals that might be a threat to you was thoroughly covered in the marine biology session. Learning urine was a good first aid for those receiving a jellyfish sting was cool. At what other time could you pee on a buddy and he would thank you?

Oceanography was interesting. The diver should know about tides, underwater currents, waterfalls, and the chill factors. Every year in the San Juan Islands, we would lose divers. Most deaths happened because of panic, and others were due to inexperience in working with Mother Nature. She is often unforgiving.

One of the most important safety rules is, "plan your dive and dive your plan." When and where do I dive and when and where will I be getting out of the water. Diving from a boat, with no one in the boat, can be scary. Divers should always swim in a direction so if the tide changes it will bring you back to your starting position. This requires you to study the tide books in your location. It can be an awful painful and long swim just to get back to your boat. I know!

First aid was easy. Both Joe and I had taken these classes in our respective school districts. We did practice retrieving a diver that passed out in the sea. CPR can be administered in both areas.

The several days we spent covering physics and physiology were, to my way of thinking, the most practical. Learning the basic laws of physics was easy. We had not thought about their application for divers. Ignorance may be blissful, but bliss under water is not what divers wish for.

Our first scolding from our instructor, or should I say warning, was, "The first thirty-three feet in diving are the most dangerous." Why? The pressure outside our body is twice that of the pressure inside our body at that depth. When wearing a tank we equalize the pressure. That is what we are supposed to do. If, however, we hold our breath and head for the surface, our lungs may have to double in size to hold this air. Rather than have the usual ten pints of air, we now have twenty pints of air. The diver could rupture a lung. Not a pretty picture.

Wetsuit squeezes can also be deadly. When you are descending, the small air bubbles in the wetsuit compress. Your weight belt could slide off your hips, down your legs, and over your fins. Without the weight, the diver could shoot to the surface with dire consequences. I found out the hard way about dropping a weight belt. If you tighten up your belt under water, you will also find out that upon reaching the surface you feel like you are being cut in half as the bubbles in your suit have expanded to twice their normal size.

Without delving into the basic laws of physics and principles, I'll discuss three extremely important topics: squeezes, bends, and the jollies.

I was enjoying an afternoon at the Islander Lopez when two men entered the building. They were looking for me. I didn't need to ask them what they wanted. I knew they were scared, and rightly so. Their eyes were almost closed, and the area around their eyes was turning black.

They had been diving off the south end of Lopez Island, without enough training and experience. They were experiencing face mask squeezes. Their eyeballs were steadily being pulled into their masks. They did not know how to clear the mask, and the pressure inside was not equal to the outside pressure. The mask was starting to crush into their faces. A quick blowing of air into their masks would have solved the problem.

After the pain hit them, they rose quickly to the surface and asked an islander for help. He referred them to me. By the time they traveled the length of the island, they were suffering from headaches, and their eyes looked nasty. I contacted the medics on the island and they contacted a seaplane operator. They were flown to a Seattle hospital.

The young divers phoned me that night to let me know their vision was returning. They would be okay. They also said they learned their lesson and would sign up for scuba instruction. Gee! It sounded like two fellows I knew.

Squeezes can occur anywhere in the human body air pockets may be found such as the ears, lungs, and sinuses.

There are several external body sites squeezes are problems. We are aware of face mask squeezes. The wetsuits also are filled with a multitude of tiny air pockets, filled with nitrogen. Descending decreases the size of the bubbles. When putting on the weight belt, it should fit tight to your hips. Even at thirty feet you can feel the belt getting looser, which would be a good time to tighten it. The diver does not want the belt slipping off, with a belt gone, and the incredible buoyancy of the suit, you may shoot to the surface.

Now, let's talk about the internal air pockets. Sinuses can be affected whether descending or ascending. Bad colds or sinus infections can, and probably will, cause you problems. If you feel any type of pressure on your sinuses, or feel as if you will be getting a headache, stop. Hold your nose and blow. Some of my friends would take out their regulators and yell. Sounds funny underwater.

The worst sinus squeezes are what we call the reverse squeezes. The diver may have spent some time on the bottom and is almost out of air. He starts to ascend when, all at once, he has this terrific headache. Recognizing the problem, he tries all the ways of clearing the plug to no avail. He has to ascend. The pain gets worse and worse closer to the surface. If he or she is lucky all that comes out is the plug and a little blood. It could well include the sinus linings.

The ear squeezes are usually caused by a blockage in the Eustachian tube, which runs from the back of the throat to the ear. Holding your nose and blowing usually unblocks the plug. My very bad experience with this squeeze is located in a later chapter about hydroplane racing in Coeur d'Alene.

Lung squeezes may be deadly. Rupturing the alveoli, grape-like sacs that make up the lungs, causes pnuemothorax. This is where air enters into the body cavity and causes collapse of the lung. All these squeezes are preventable. Equalize, equalize, equalize.

Anyways, I think I'll stick to my wife's squeezes. Much more fun!

Now onto the bends. Nitrogen is a very interesting gas. While it makes up about 80 percent of the air we breathe it has little use in our bodies. One of its characteristics is it easily absorbs into the body tissues and organs. It does not easily dissolve back into the atmosphere.

When diving, nitrogen enters the blood stream, muscles, lungs, brain tissues, and other vital body parts. Nitrogen in the body is like soda in a Coke can. You can shake it and nothing happens. But if you shake the can and open it you will have Coke everywhere. If you stay down too long, when diving, or surface too fast, this will cause the nitrogen to form bubbles. When ascending with these bubbles, they increase in size and can cause great harm to the diver. The phenomenon was originally named Caisson's Disease. It occurred in tunnel workers and miners. After scuba diving it became known as Diver's Disease or commonly the "bends."

There are basically three types of bends: skin bends, muscle or organ bends, and nerve hits. The nerve hit occurs in the brain and catastrophic things may occur, usually resulting in death. The bubbles rupture every cell around them. First aid includes laying the patient down, wrapping him in blankets, and sending for a doctor. Also, contact the nearest recompression chamber and police for transportation.

I experienced the skin bends only once and none of the others. Thank heavens! Knowing one kind of bend may be followed by another kind is exceedingly scary. I was lying on the deck, covered with a blanket, and I felt like my skin was being covered by bugs. I itched all over. I had no pain in my joints nor was I dizzy or nauseous. The crew and I talked about having me descend to the bottom, which would reduce the size of the bubbles thus making it less painful for me. If I went back to the bottom, I would also have more bottom time, which would mean a longer decompression when I returned to the surface and perhaps a greater danger of joint bends or nerve hits. We would wait it out.

Presently, there are chambers all around Puget Sound, Canada and Spokane, Washington. The chambers come in all sizes, from a one person tube to a much larger chamber that is able to hold the diver and several medical personnel. The chamber, under pressure, takes you back down to the deepest depth you were diving. It's up to the diver to keep excellent records of his dives. Records should include how deep, how much time at the depth, how many tanks were used and how much time elapsed between dives. The experienced diver knows how to use the U.S. Navy's Diving Tables and hopefully uses them to his advantage. Keep good logs.

What other fun characteristics does nitrogen have that we should look out for? Well, the second one that comes to mind, and it is one that I can relate to, is termed "jollies."

Several years after completing the class, a group of us were sitting around the office at Skin Diver's Cove when Bob Stanton came in announcing that an early Chinese vase had been discovered at the base of Blakely Rocks. He asked if any of us would be interested in diving the following day to see if there were more vases to be found. Three of us jumped at the chance and the next day we motored to the rock.

On the way out, Bob asked if we had ever seen "Old Red" or "Scarface." We hadn't. He told us we were in for a treat. We would see it on the way to the bottom. It usually hung out in the same old cave. Bob said it was the biggest octopus he had ever seen, and he had seen plenty. We were more excited than ever.

Bob and I partnered and took off first. We were only about seventy-five feet deep when Bob pointed to a large cave. Swimming over I saw two of the biggest, piercing yellow eyes I had ever seen. I backed up! Although most of him was hidden in the cave, his tentacles were huge. I was in no mood to pick an argument with this leviathan.

Alongside the mantel was a nasty, ragged scar. Bob thought it was the work of some thoughtless diver who attempted to spear him. From a safe distance we watched him with much interest.

Bob pointed to the bottom and led the way down. I'm not sure what depth we were at, but Bob began to swim around and around in tight, little circles. He was not going up or down. I slowly descended to his depth, and swam very slowly up behind him. Taking the top of his tank in one hand and the bottom of the tank in the other, we continued to swim in little circles, ascending slowly. At sixty feet, Bob began to turn to see who or what had the back of his tank. I let go, swam to his front and pointed to the surface. We reached the surface, swam to the boat and climbed in. I explained what had happened and Bob said he had no memory of it. He was probably too tired from the night before and should not have had that last martini. We never did find any other vases, but we often returned to the rock to show off and say hello to Old Red.

The reason I used the term martini in recounting the story is because divers and scientists have come up with their own law of physics. The effects of the jollies they call "Martini's Law," and it states that for every fifty feet a diver dives is like drinking one very large martini. Therefore, at one hundred feet, it would be two martinis and so on. The only solution is to bring the person to the surface very slowly. Many people, who have no partners, die by staying on the bottom until their air ran out.

A famous aviator once commented flying was hours of boredom followed by minutes of pure terror. I believe diving can be like that even among experienced divers. You might be out for a Sunday afternoon fun dive, perhaps you are taking pictures, collecting specimens, and spearfishing or what have you, when all hell breaks loose. A rip tide changes direction or you are caught in an underwater waterfall or experience the sting of the deadly sea wasp. Getting your mask ripped off by an octopus or reaching the surface and finding your boat missing is really exciting. Believe me, it can happen!

After our classes were behind us, Joe and I assisted Bob Stanton, with our new friend Fred Laister, in helping others become certified divers. With Bob, it was particularly exhilarating to help train the engineers of the Boeing Company, who built the hydrofoils (The Puget Sound and Catalina Fliers).Following these experiences I started the Washington School of Diving and later became a commercial sea food diver and dive boat owner with my wife, Beverly.

Chapter 3

~~~~~~

Prop Dodgers and Crab Scratchers

UPON COMPLETION OF our NAUI course, our entire graduating class was asked to join the Puget Sound Prop Dodgers. Our meetings were held at Skin Diver's Cove in Bellevue, Washington.

Most of our meetings lasted one hour and we always spent time over a cold one. The main agenda items, almost every time, included when and where we would dive next. We let the non-divers in our group worry about such things as food.

We loved our club dives and get-togethers. Our families would always attend as well as non-diving friends. We had as many as eighty people attend one of the functions. Most of our trips were day dives, but we could also be found on weekend campouts. The children loved spending a few nights in a tent away from the hustle and bustle of town.

Our favorite spot was Odlin Park on Lopez Island. Located on the north side of the island, Odlin was a five minute drive from the ferry dock. Besides food and drink, we took all sorts of camping gear, generators and air compressors (to fill our tanks). We often took the family pets as well.

Diving at the park was a ho-hum experience. There was hardly any marine life aside from the occasional crab, starfish, etc. The sandy beaches, shallow water and surrounding woods were a child's paradise. The children could wade a long way out and the water did not go over their heads. No rip tides existed. An old cannon, pointed at Shaw Island, was a great place to play war. I don't know how many times our children fended off pirates with that cannon.

Dale Rarry, our campground host, was friendly to us, but a bit feisty to others who did not follow the rules. He single-handedly chased some bikers off the island. Actually it was Dale and a twelve gauge shot gun. Over a bottle of bourbon, "Gilligan" would recount his exploits while working on the railroads. Every visitor, and those that knew Dale, called him "Gilligan." Even after he passed away, our friends always referred to Lopez as "Gilligan's Island."

The Skin Diver Cove's club was named the Prop Dodgers, a well respected and fun group. The Prop Dodgers had a membership of sixty divers plus their families. The Kent Valley Crab Scratchers were not recognized as a diver's club. The Crab Scratchers were not all divers and families, but a group of patrons of the Colonial House Tavern in Kent, Washington. The later club had seven divers. We did have a grand time being members of both clubs.

One day while camping at Odlin, we saw a small sailboat enter the bay, luff the sails, and drop its anchor. After stowing the sails, a couple jumped into a small boat, called a dingy, and headed for shore. They tied their dingy to the wharf and strolled over to our campsite. We began to talk, and we asked them to join our little group. Around four o' clock, we drove them to town to get supplies and have a beer. On our return, the kids were all excited. The sailboat had taken off by itself, and floated around the tip of the island. Our visitors were beside themselves.

We grabbed Gilligan's boat, which had an engine, and took off after the boat. Less than an hour later we caught up to the boat. No one was on board, and her anchor was dragging through the water. Thank heavens the water was calm and there was no major tidal change.

We raised the anchor, fastened the sailboat to Gilligan's little skiff and motored back to the bay. There was no damage to the sailboat, but it could have run onto the rocks. Ed, the captain, and his wife were greatly relieved that their boat was safe. They had anchored the boat in twenty-five feet of water and let out thirty feet of anchor and chain. They did not realize how different the tides were in our area. The water had risen ten feet. Not what they had expected. The rising tide had merely pulled the anchor off the bottom.

Ed and his wife visited our group many times after that event, and one day he made a confession. He told us that he was the commodore of one of Seattle's best know yacht clubs. He swore us to secrecy. Ed's gone now, but I'm honoring his request by not telling you his last name or to what club he belonged.

Chapter 4

~~~~~~~~~~~~~~~~~~~~~~~~~~~~

Divers Clubs

THERE ARE MANY excellent diving clubs throughout the northwest and the rest of the United States including the Prop Dodgers, The Boeing Seahorses, Northwest Divers, and the Mud Sharks were perhaps the best known dive clubs in the U.S., if not the world. These clubs were located in Seattle. The Boeing Seahorses were, at one time, the largest dive club in the world.

The members of these clubs were very proficient in spearfishing. Gary Keffler won a world cup in Rio. Why then had our little club, the Prop Dodgers, dared to take on these giants? Stupidity comes to mind. We did, however, want to learn from the best. We also enjoyed their friendship.

A typical spearfishing contest consisted of a two-to-three-hour dive in the morning, without using scuba equipment, and then a two-to-three-hour break for lunch. The afternoon was spent spearing fish with scuba gear. At the end of the day, the fish were counted, weighed and measured. Awards were given, and if any records were made, they were recorded for the winter awards ceremony. In the years that followed, I received two awards. The skates that I brought in were record size and weights.

On a beautiful day in August, we met at Fidalgo Island, which is north of Seattle and Whidbey Island. We would dive in an area known as the Narrows. This river-like body of water ran between Fidalgo Island and the north side of Whidbey Island. Speeds of ten knots were not uncommon in this channel. Slower boats could not fight their way up current much less a diver trying to swim.

This particular morning, the weather was beautiful and we waited for the whistle to blow and send us on our hunt. I chose a rock wall on the north side of Canoe Island. This small island is in the channel and nearer the Fidalgo side than the Whidbey Island side. On reaching the site, I took a deep breath and, carrying my lance and fishing stringer, dove to the bottom. I was west of Canoe and I came across a reef loaded with ling cod. I saw a huge ling above my head. He was sitting on top of the reef. I started up and was immediately pushed back down. I was caught in an underwater waterfall. I turned and followed the reef back to where I began. I was about out of air when I reached the surface. My lungs were hurting, but I found the float board I had come out on and I quickly climbed atop it. I pulled up the little anchor that kept my board from being dragged away by the tide and headed back to shore. When the tide was almost non-existent I returned and had a fairly good fishing day. The most important rule of plan your dive and dive your plan had a special meaning for me that day. I should have read the tide book. If I wouldn't have fought my way out of the waterfall when I did I would have been swept down into two hundred feet of water.

While I never won a spearfishing contest, my living room did have, on its walls, two Washington State records for the biggest skates caught. The skates, a relative of rays and sharks, have large wings, which taste like scallops and are often sold to the unsuspecting as ocean scallops.

The Puget Sound Skin Divers' Council eventually realized how wasteful it was to the fish and harmful to the ecology of the area. They no longer support spearfishing contests.

Spearfishing was not the only entertainment afforded the dive club members. Titlow Beach is in an area near where the famous "Galloping Gertie" bridge collapsed into the Tacoma Narrows. It was at the marina where our annual Octopus Grapple took place. Puget Sound has the largest octopuses anywhere in the world.

We dove without tanks in the morning and with them in the afternoon. These events occurred using the buddy system. The octopuses were huge and, while not aggressive, they could hang onto a diver until the diver ran out of air. They were hard to get out of caves, especially with their very large tentacles grasping the cave walls. Unlike what the movies may show us, an octopus has no power of constriction. They cannot squeeze you to death.

To get them out of their holes, some divers would squirt bleach into the caves. Having very sensitive skin, bleach usually would drive them out. Our team did not like that method of extricating them from their lair. We thought it more humane to tickle them with a long baby-bottle brush. They didn't like it but it didn't hurt them. Once out of the cave, we would grab them and head for the surface. More than once, I had my mask taken off and, on a few occasions, had my regulator jerked out of my mouth. That's why we dove with a partner.

We kept all our catches in huge aquariums until the end of the day. They were weighed and sent to the Seattle and Point Defiance Aquariums, but most were released back to their homes.

It was after one of these events that a new diver, from our club, wanted to see the remains of "Gertie." Bob Stanton, Sally, who was a new SCUBA student, and I swam north to a spot under the new Tacoma Narrows bridge.

We began our descent to where some of the wreckage remains. We never made it to the bottom. The current began to pick up and if we didn't get out of there soon, we surely would have had problems. Having a novice along was not going to help. We did not dare take a chance swimming straight to the surface. The Narrows was famous for whirlpools and being sucked down into deep water was not an option. With Bob on one side and me on the other, we forced Sally to the sand. We were about halfway to the surface. In the process of pulling our new diver up the steep, sandy bottom safe zone, Sally lost one of her fins. Hugging the bottom, Bob pulled her toward land. Getting as close to the sand as possible, I kept Sally's rear end down. The fast water flowing over her kept the three of us from being swept away. It seemed to take forever, but we finally pulled ourselves onto the shore where we lay for several minutes. Looking around, we found ourselves about two miles away from the marina. Bob left his gear on the beach and walked back for help. Our dive club members were quick to respond. They helped us carry our equipment back to Titlow Beach. We were very thankful that all ended well.

Chapter 5

A Weekend at Dewatto Bay

DEWATTO BAY, MORE a cove than a bay, is located on Hoods Canal, due north and west of Seattle.

The waters leaving Hood's Canal enter Puget Sound. It is here, at the mouth, that the world's longest floating bridge can be found. Bangor Naval Base is located several miles inside the canal's entrance. Bangor houses nuclear submarines equipped with Trident missiles. While our boat could reach speeds of forty-five knots, we could never keep up with those "boomers." We tried on many occasions to get close to them. No luck!

Hoods Canal was also known for its oysters and excellent diving. It was for these reasons we were headed for the cabin of Wes and Martha Stevens. Wes and Martha were members of our Crab Scratchers club. They enjoyed the water and their little cabin in the woods. Their cabin was within walking distance to the bay.

Six adults and seven children would be the guests of the Stevens. Wes had invited a few of our diving club members for the weekend. We were looking forward to the friendship, the exhilarating diving and the ample supply of drinks and gourmet seafood.

The twenty-by-twenty-four foot board and bat cabin was just that a cabin. The chimney bricks looked as if they would topple at any moment and the board and bat had not seen paint for years. Inside the cabin everything was clean and open. There was only one enclosed room, the bathroom. Thank heavens! It had a toilet and a lime-stained, claw-footed bathtub. The main room served as the kitchen, dining room and bedroom. We were all glad we had brought our air mattresses, down sleeping bags and tents. The weather had turned cold. The children would sleep in the house in their sleeping bags.

One large, black cast iron, ornately carved stove would serve to cook our meals, provide warmth and hot water for the bathtub.

Martha explained how the tub worked. First, you needed to bring four buckets of well water into the house. Secondly, you poured the contents into a copper boiler attached on the stove. A system of pipes went through the stove, out the back, through a hole in the wall and into the tub. Third, you were to bring one bucket of very cold water to the bathtub and set it on the floor. When steam came out of the tap, you mixed the very, very hot water with the cold. There was always a fear of being par-boiled. I don't believe any of our crew decided to try it. We did find a use for the tub later.

Arriving Friday afternoon, we had time to stow all the food, clothing, diving gear and toys. We put up our tents and then wandered into the house. Wes said that we should let the ladies talk and the children play, and we should walk down to the bay. It was only a half-mile away. Fifteen minutes later we saw the bay. Next to a small dock a well-worn but sturdy rowboat was tied. In the middle of the bay, was a dilapidated barge. A weather-beaten shelter was nailed to the deck. Alongside the barge, and tied by its painter, drifted a skiff.

Yes! Art would be home. His skiff was tied to the barge, smoke exited the chimney, and steam erupted from the aft portion of the deck. Perfect timing.

Art was a recluse. It was rumored that he had moved to this remote area fifty-some years ago after killing a man in the Midwest. He never talked about it and we never asked.

Art did odd jobs for the few who lived nearby, but his main source of income came from the sea. He fished, collected and shucked oysters, and kept his crab and shrimp pots in the canal.

The locals had dubbed Art the *Mayor of Dewatto Bay*. Art took great pleasure in being called Mr. Mayor.

We jumped into the boat and rowed toward the barge. Halfway there, Art spotted us and gave us the customary, "Ahoy!" A wave of his arm let us know we were welcome. Had we been strangers, I'm not sure what his response would have been. Art did recognize his old friend Wes.

Art seldom went to town, which was nearly forty miles away. His needs were few. Mainly he shopped for flour, sugar and coffee. Selling crabs for seventy-five cents a pound didn't leave him with much money to purchase whiskey, which he dearly loved.

Once on the deck, Wes unbuttoned his coat and brought out a half-gallon bottle of Black Velvet, which he handed to

"His Honor." Art's eyes popped open as he reached for the bottle. With a big smile, he darted into his shack and returned with empty jelly jars. He generously filled each of our jars and proceeded to the stern of the barge where we had seen the steam earlier. The steam was coming from a huge cast iron pot. Art scooped up big, dark-red, boiled prawns from the tub. Returning with heaping bowls of this delicacy, he said, "Dig in, gentlemen."

After an hour of peeling and eating prawns, chatting, and drinking whiskey, we thought we had better head back to the cabin and our families.

Returning to the dock, we all expressed our concerns about this eighty-year old man. He lived on the water, in all kinds of weather, climbed and descended that ladder, rowed his skiff up and down the canal and he didn't know how to swim.

The cool reception we received on our return to the cabin was somewhat nullified when Wes held up a mesh bag crammed with ten pounds of delicious, Hood Canal prawns, which we had purchased from Art. Our price, from the "mayor" was $7.50.

That evening was spent visiting. Wes and Martha were great people with senses of humor to match. Wes was quite a character. He had been highly recruited by all the, then, Pac-10 universities, for his skills in football. While shorter than I, Wes was much larger in girth. Barrel-chested and with strong legs and thighs, he was particularly crafty at running over defensive linemen.

Wes didn't fear anything. Anything human that is. Well, maybe Martha on occasion. Martha gave up trying to get him to change light bulbs. He was afraid of electricity.

Before heading off to bed, Martha told us what had occurred at her home prior to Thanksgiving. Martha had purchased a live, thirty pound tom turkey. Before she left the house to go shopping, she instructed Wes to kill the bird and leave the carcass outside near their mudroom. On her return, she would pluck it, clean it, and have it ready for dinner the next day. She would return in a couple of hours. Martha left Wes with the turkey and a well-honed, short-handled axe.

Upon her exit, Wes strolled outside. He looked at the turkey, looked at the axe, shook his head, and walked back into the house. Pouring a double-shot of Jim Beam, Wes calculated his next move. Putting down the glass, Wes left the house and headed for the turkey. One look at the turkey, and it was back into the house for another double-shot.

It is impossible to tell how many trips Wes made back into the house. When Martha returned, she saw a most remarkable sight. The tom was tied, by the neck, to a fir tree. Wes was standing ten feet away, blindfolded. In his hands, he held his son's bow and arrows. Arrows were all over the yard, in the trees but not one in the turkey.

Martha made Wes take off his blindfold, put down the bow and arrows, and follow her into the house. She put him to bed on the davenport. Martha then returned to the turkey and quickly dispatched him. Wes just didn't have the heart to hurt that old turkey.

On Saturday morning, we decided that a rowboat and skiff did not hold enough people for all of us to dive on the same day. We drew lots to see who would dive Saturday and who would dive on Sunday. Walt James, our next door neighbor, and I would dive off the row boat, skippered by Wes. Club members and fellow teachers, Dick and Gail, would dive in the skiff with Art as captain.

Wes rowed us to an area where he had caught rock fish. If they were still in the area they would make a delicious dinner. We were looking forward to finding a reef or rocky outcropping.

Upon reaching the dive site, Walt and I did a back roll into the canal. The water was cold and slack (no current). The cold, seawater cascaded down the inside of our wetsuits. That is a good way to quickly get rid of a hangover. Wide awake we descended. The water here was sixty feet deep and the visibility was clear.

Walt had completed his NAUI training three months earlier but he was still not a strong swimmer. He was smart and followed the rules. Walt took the lead. We came to rest in a pretty desolate area. Walt motioned for an equipment check. Upon completing the task the okay signs were flashed.

We had not landed on the reef but in an area divers call a desert. Seemingly barren, life here was most unusual: sea pens and sea whips (strange looking animals that looked like plants – some pencil shaped and some looking like feathery writing quills), sole and flounder, multi-armed sea stars and rat fish. Walt hated rat fish. Perhaps it was the nasty spine in front of their dorsal fin or perhaps it was those rat-like teeth, which could crush a clam in one bite. The rat fish is not aggressive, but Walt wanted no part of the one we had just seen. He motioned me to move up the hill toward the reef.

Traveling slowly up the incline, Walt stopped and began waving furiously. He pointed to his left, the opposite side from where I was swimming. I swam quickly to the side where he was pointing. A large octopus was undulating across the sand, hunting for its favorite food, crabs. The mantle was camouflaged by matching the surrounding terrain. With its five-foot long tentacles, it was a magnificent specimen. What a prize catch!

I pushed Walt back and threw him my spear gun, fish stringer and goody bag. He deftly retrieved them.

I grabbed the octopus, jamming my thumbs into its siphons. He could not jet-propel himself away. I turned the animal upside down so I could observe its parrot-like beak. No Puget Sound diver, to my knowledge, had ever been bitten and I didn't want to be the first. We headed for the surface. Looking up, I saw the bottom of Wes's boat. He had been hovering above our bubbles. It was also snowing.

On reaching the surface, Walt and I threw the octopus into the boat.

Wes yelled, "What in the hell?" Then we heard the splash, and the boat rocked. Walt raced around the bow and I the stern. Wes was in the water. He wanted no "damn" part of that creature.

We threw our gear into the boat. Walt climbed over the port rail and I the starboard (to steady the boat). I'm not sure if it was the cold water or our assurances of safety, but Wes finally let us haul him aboard. Not an easy task for a man of his size.

Walt rowed. I sat in the bow with the octopus. Wes, drenching wet, sat shivering in the stern.

Twenty minutes later, Dick and Gail popped to the surface with stringers of rock cod. They slid into Art's skiff, and we all headed for shore.

Thankfully Martha had a warm fire waiting for us. We were all chilled to the bone.

An hour later, Wes, now dressed, sat rocking, drinking and enjoying the moment. After several beers, Wes excused himself and headed for the bathroom. A loud yell soon followed. Then the bathroom door flew open. Wes streaked by, ran out the door, and headed for the woods.

We rushed to the bathroom and saw the cause of his terror. Our octopus was attempting to crawl out of the lime-stained tub. Two tentacles had already touched the floor. I guess we should have told Wes that we were keeping our future dinner in the tub.

What a feast we had that evening. We ate fried cod, oysters on the half-shell, steamed clams, boiled prawns, and the mantle of the octopus. Mayor Art was our honored guest. We saved the rest of the octopus to be smoked by a company in Redmond, Washington.

Sunday morning passed quickly. The other group of divers spent their morning in the water.

While the divers were busy, several of us headed for the beach to pick oysters. I placed a bucket behind me. I didn't want it to get in the way of my shucking. Minutes passed, and turning to check my progress, I found an empty bucket and my three-year-old son, Jamie, with a big smile on his face. He had eaten everyone I had shucked. They did not make him sick and to this day he still loves raw oysters.

By noon we had packed and said our thanks and goodbyes. What a weekend it was.

Rat Fish

Chapter 6

~~~~~~

Tidal Wave

ON A BEAUTIFUL March evening, our club decided to participate in a night dive off the Edmonds ferry boat dock. Just north of the dock, one hundred feet off shore, lay the remains of an old, sunken dry dock. It was a fun place to visit in the daytime. At night, everything would be spectacular.

We put on our gear, checked that our underwater lights were working and walked into the water. A short swim, and a dive to a depth of fifty feet, put us near our target. Everything was quiet and dark. We switched on our lights, and the dry dock became alive with waving sea anemones. Fish were sleeping, and with no eyelids, their eyes were bright and shiny. We crept up on them and patted them on the heads.

One of our dive team gave a signal for us to turn off our lights. It was more than dark, it was pitch black. We sat for a few seconds to allow our eyes to adjust to the lack of light. We approached the sea anemones and squeezed their stalks. Sparks shot from the top of their stomachs. What a sight! The bio-luminescence of an aquatic protozoan known as *noctiluca* was responsible for the sparks. When agitated, the little creatures would glow. I was very aware of this little guy. At night, on Puget Sound, with the boat engine running, a trail of luminescence would follow in the boat's wake. On shore, my children, Jamie and Dana, would do what they called the *noctiluca* stomp. Sparks would fly on the beach in rhythm to their little dance.

Our group leader motioned we travel single file all around the sunken dock. It was great! As the divers swam, the sparks flew in all directions off our bodies and especially off our fins. The divers were encased in an eerie glow. We spent about thirty minutes being awed by the experience. It was time to surface and end our wonderful dive.

Up on the beach, our spouses were frantically trying to figure out some way to contact us. They even resorted to throwing rocks in the water to no avail. They had been listening to the car radios.

On Friday, March 27, 1964, the Great Alaskan earthquake had occurred at 5:36 p.m. While it only lasted five minutes, it was the most powerful earthquake in the United States and North American history. We had heard about the quake shortly after it happened, but we were diving on Saturday, and Alaska was a long way off.

What we did not know was the earthquake had created a tsunami (tidal wave) and it was heading in our direction. Our spouses were beside themselves.

Near the end of our dive, we noticed that the sea animals were awake and darted about as if very excited. The current had picked up and it was moving faster than our tide book had shown. We thought we had nothing to worry about, we were about finished anyway. We followed the leader to the ferry dock, stood up, and looked around. We were standing in the middle where the ferry boats came in. Our heads were out of water. The ferry needed deeper water than this. We had spit out our regulators and were trying to make some sense out of the situation when one of our members heard a lady yell to get out of the water. We walked to shore and listened to several people talking at the same time. They explained a huge wall of water was rushing down the Pacific Coast.

We took off our gear and walked over to where the car radios were blaring. The wall of water wouldn't affect us. Instead of coming into Puget Sound, it rushed down the coast toward California. As the tidal wave moved down the coast, our water was pulled toward the tidal flow. The water had dropped drastically in Puget Sound, but no one was hurt.

Many people were killed in the tsunami. In Prince William Sound, a twenty-seven foot tsunami wave destroyed the village of Chenega. Twenty-three of the sixty-eight people who lived there were killed. Sixteen people died in Oregon and California, and millions of dollars in damages had occurred.

Looking back, I guess we sort-of almost dove in a tsunami.

Chapter 7

~~~~~~~~~~~~~~~~~~~~~~~~~~~

Killer Whales-Part 1

THE BEST DIVER I ever partnered with was Fred Laister. Fred knew every rock, reef, and shipwreck in Hoods Canal, Puget Sound, and the San Juan Islands. Fred also owned property on Lopez Island. Safety was always foremost when I dove with him.

Fred approached me one afternoon with a suggestion we dive near Port Orchard. Many purple-hinged rock scallops could be found there. The weather would be great and the water was calm.

We left the Des Moines Boat Basin early Saturday morning in my Sabrecraft. Two hours later we dropped the hook in front of a rock cliff. Coves on both sides of us would offer protection against strong currents and the waves from passing boats.

Fred entered the water first, as was his custom, and hand-over-hand pulled himself down the anchor line to the bottom. He secured the anchor between two large boulders. With the task completed, Fred pushed the purge valve on his regulator. Bubbles erupted, drifted to the surface and burst. It was a signal for me to enter the water and descend to where he waited for me.

The water, this day, was dark and silty. Poor visibility.

Encrusted with sponges, sea anemones, sea stars and barnacles, our wall stood before us. Beginning at the bottom we slowly crisscrossed the face of the wall, cutting the adductor muscles from the shells of the scallops and popping the delicious morsels into our goody bags.

On reaching the surface, we learned we only had five scallops, not nearly enough for the party we had planned. The current was picking up, but we agreed to return to the bottom and swim into the lee-side cove.

We found scallops everywhere. Our bags were beginning to get heavy with the weight of them. We were far back in the cove, but we still had plenty of air, we thought. My gauge read five hundred pounds. This was one-sixth the amount of a full aluminum tank.

We began our ascent. Something strange and foreboding lay above our heads. It was blurry, with concentric lines. A giant web! Not a web, but a net. It was the thickest, heaviest net I'd ever seen. It was at least two inches thick. We would not have time to cut through it.

Fred pointed to himself and then to me. He wanted me to follow him and do exactly as he did. He approached the net and rolled over on his back. The goody bags kept our rears down. To lose a weight belt here would be disastrous. The buoyancy of our wetsuits would press us into the net. Moving anywhere would be impossible. We would shortly run out of air.

Slowly, we edged our way toward the open water and freedom. Minutes passed and our air was running out! The net began curving upward. We spotted open water, pushed off the net, expelled the last of our air and shot to the surface.

The net was attached to a series of buoys that circled this cove. How had we missed all this? We swam to one of buoys where a sign warned, "No Trespassing Killer Whale." With deep sighs and a shake of our heads, we silently contemplated what could have happened.

We swam to the boat, stowed our gear, put the scallop muscles on ice and motored back to the marina. We found out that the pen was designed to hold Namu, the first orca to be sold to an aquarium. Namu would be held here until transported to his new home. I never believed in capturing orcas after that experience.

Chapter 8

Killer Whales - Part 2

LIVING AND PLAYING in the San Juan Islands awarded us with hundreds of encounters with killer whales, *Orcinus orca,* usually from the safe environs of a boat.

Fishing on the Salmon Banks was a particularly good spot to catch halibut, salmon, and ling cod. The killer whales knew this. Next to seals, sea lions and other whales, the fish were a great food source.

The San Juan Channel is located between Lopez Island, on the east, and San Juan Island, on the west. It is four miles wide and a main avenue for orcas to reach the Salmon Banks.

It was in this channel that Fred Laister and I had come to hunt for ling cod. These toothy fish often reached weights of eighty pounds. We would be happy to spear two ten pounders.

After securely anchoring the boat, we dove to the bottom and was about to start spearfishing when I signaled Fred that I was going to return to the surface. I had to retrieve my fish stringer, which I had carelessly left on the outside swim step of the boat.

I reached the surface. Across the channel, I spotted water spouts. These, of course, came from a whale or dolphin. The question that flashed through my mind was which was it? I was not happy to see the black whales with the white markings. A killer whale pod! They were headed in our direction. Divers dressed in black look a lot like they belong to the orca's food group.

Seeing Fred's bubbles, I followed them down to where he was sitting on the bottom, patiently waiting for me. I motioned for him to surface. Once there Fred asked, "What's going on?"

I started to point across the channel when I felt very strange. Something was happening that sent chills down my neck and back. Turning around slowly, I looked into an eye the size of a small dinner plate. The whale was six feet away, too close for us to make it to the boat.

I closed my eyes, and waited. Opening my eyes and looking around, I was relieved to see our company had left. I heard Fred laughing.

As we climbed into the boat, Fred told me what I had seen was a young pilot whale. This whale had also spotted the orcas and being frightened and smart, had crossed to the outside of the channel.

Fred and I sat in the boat for a long time after the killer whales had left the area. We were taking no chances. The ling cods would just have to wait.

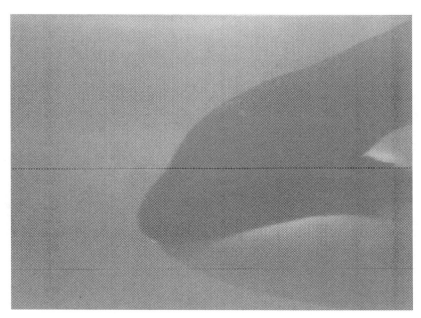

Killer Whale

Chapter 9

Sharks, Rays and Skates

THE MOST FREQUENT question posed to divers is, "Have you ever had any encounters with sharks?" The answer by most salt water divers is invariably yes! If you spend any time at all in the oceans, seas or bays, you are bound to run into these denizens.

Ancient sharks, such as *megaladon*, have roamed the seas millions of years ago, and their relatives can be found today in fresh and salt water and in warm and cold environments. They may be egg layers or give live birth. Being cartilaginous they are not related to boney fish. They all have one thing in common; they are born to eat.

The most common sharks in Puget Sound and in the San Juan Islands are dogfish, six gill, seven gill and the brown catshark. The shark most often caught by fishermen is the dogfish. This shark is very aggressive and often travels in packs, much to the chagrin of one of our divers.

We were beginning to lose sunlight when my partner motioned she wanted to head for shore, a little less than one hundred feet away. I pointed out a big rock cod that was attempting to hide behind a few scattered rocks. I handed her the fish stringer and motioned for her to head in. I would soon follow. I shot the fish with a lance and returned to our original position. In less than five minutes, I came across my buddy. She was standing on the bottom and there was only two feet of water above her head. She was almost to shore. She had four unwanted dogfish circling her. They were not after her, but they did want the fish on the stringer. She was batting at them with the stringer. By the wild look in her eyes, I knew she was scared. I, Sir Galahad, rushed to her aid. Smacking the sharks with my lance, they fled. We swam to shore. It was not Sir Galahad that she called me. Gail was mad at me for weeks for leaving her alone.

There have been reports of great white sharks on the Washington coast due to the changing weather patterns. The body of a great white was found on a Vashon Island beach. A mako shark was caught off Friday Harbor in the San Juan Islands and basking sharks have been spotted in Puget Sound, off Point Defiance in Tacoma. All are very dangerous!

While ocean fishing off the Washington coast, we often caught the very blue Salmon shark. We were jigging one day for king salmon when a seven-foot blue hit four of our herrings. The shark also managed to entangle another five fishermen's lines. What a mess! Combining our efforts, we hauled the shark to the stern of the boat, where the captain shot him. It took a long time to untangle the lines and hooks. I never saw a salmon shark in the Puget Sound area, but they can be very aggressive.

You have heard how great shark meat can taste. I've tried the shark fin soup. Yuk! If you try to prepare a fillet, remember that many sharks urinate through their skin. Wash and wash and wash before cooking and eating.

I had the opportunity of working with (not for) NASA for three years. We (aerospace educators) often had the opportunity of visiting many of their locations. One summer, we visited Cape Canaveral and Cape Kennedy. Having an afternoon off, we headed for the beach. We talked to a few locals and they told us that three reefs ran parallel to shore and one could often find interesting marine life on these reefs.

Donning my fins, face plate and snorkel, I entered the warm water of the Atlantic. I found the first series of reefs fairly devoid of life. I moved on, a little farther off shore. The water was not only warm, but very salty. Reef two had more life, but I still searched for more. I almost reached the third reef when I saw divers and swimmers heading for shore in a great hurry. One young man hollered at me that hammerheads had moved into the area. Yes they had! I think I beat most of the swimmers back to shore. So much for those barrier reefs.

While sharks can be the most chilling animals, we must remember more people die from bees, hornets, wasps and even dogs.

Skates and ray are also found in the Puget Sound and San Juan Island areas. Cousins of the sharks, these animals have large wings that stretch out from their main body. The skate has a very pointed nose, and the ray a very blunt head. The skates may be huge, wide and long. The mouth, with sharp teeth, is located on the underside of the animal. They live on small fish, like sand dabs, flounder and sole and on small crustaceans. They are beautiful swimmers. In certain areas of the world, skate fisherman skin the animal, and with circular cutters cut out chunks of meat and sell them as ocean scallops. They are tasty, but not as good as the real thing.

There is only one species of rays in the Pacific Northwest. Electric rays have been found in the northern portion of the Puget Sound. These smaller versions of the sting ray carry a mean electrical charge. The discharge will stun small prey and make gathering food easier. A strong jolt is a very good defense for the ray's protection. When in tropical water, we were taught that when you entered the water from the shore you should shuffle your feet. This scares the rays away. The stingray uses the stinger as a defense mechanism only.

Dive instructors always tell their students to buddy up. In other words, don't dive alone! I do have another view point on this. You should have a buddy for safety's sake, but then in case of a shark attack there is a fifty-fifty chance he will get your buddy instead of you. Just kidding!

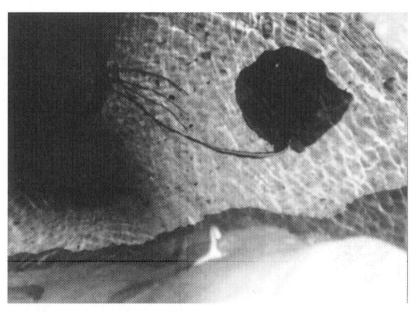

Sting Ray

Chapter 10

How Deep Should We Dive?

HOW DEEP SHOULD we dive?

Joe and I often asked ourselves this question, especially after diving on a wreck. Many wrecks were much deeper than we cared to dive. Our time was limited and we did not want to use double tanks in fear of the bends.

One Saturday afternoon, Joe and I were killing time in Skin Divers Cove. The owner showed us a bulletin from the Skin Divers' Council. A deep-water diver, who was an expert of commercial deep saturation dives, was going to present a three-hour class on rare gas diving and the physics of gases.

His name was Jon and he lived on Bainbridge Island. I decided to do a little research on him before signing up for the class.

While a student at Stanford, Jon was the first diver west of the Mississippi to cave dive. Upon completion of his engineering degree, he joined the U.S. Navy. As a lieutenant, he served in a UDT (Underwater Demolition Team) unit. The Commander and Jon's boss was Francis "Red Dog" Fane. Boy did that get my attention. Commander Fane introduced scuba to the navy and divers. Nicknamed "Red Dog" for the color of his hair, his name was a very well known to me. He started the organization of NAUI (National Association of Underwater Instructors). Joe and I both had NAUI cards, two years after the organization was started.

What really tickled me was the fact that Jon and Fane were the technical support for a television show my children loved, *Sea Hunt*.

What also intrigued me was the connection he had with another famous Seattle person, Ed Link. Link, a millionaire, was the owner-inventor of the famous Link Aviation Trainer. Mr. Link was also an avid, underwater deep dive fan. He supervised a successful four-hundred-and-thirty-feet dive off the Great Stirrup Cap in the Bahamas. Jon was one of Link's divers that spent considerable time in a portable, inflatable dwelling at great depths.

We were ready to register for this man's class immediately after reading the instructor's credentials. The class was all we thought it would be. He discussed all aspects of deep water diving, their pros and cons. He discussed the uses of blended gases and how very few people were putting the different combinations of gases together for commercial uses.

Since those days, Nitrox and Trimix have been used by countless commercial and fun divers. Nitrox replaces some of the nitrogen with more oxygen. This mixture reduces chances of getting the bends or jollies. Trimix reduces the amount of both oxygen and nitrogen and adds other gases such as argon and helium. Presently, the cost of mixed gases is extremely high and a diver must take classes and be certified to use the mixes. The training and certification may cost more than one thousand dollars.

Over a beer, Joe and I decided that we would stick with our old ways of diving.

During class, I found out Jon was only two months older than I. What he had accomplished was remarkable. At the end of class, Jon told us that his dad had told him never to go into the aviation business, it was much too dangerous. Oh, Jon's dad was Charles "Lucky Lindy" Lindbergh. Jon Morrow Lindberg was the second son of the Lindberghs.

Chapter 11

The Diamond Cup

IN THE 60S and 70s, hydroplane racing was a large spectator sport in North Idaho. The Diamond Cup, for unlimited hydroplanes, was held on Coeur d'Alene Lake.

It was on a visit to my mother's I stopped at one of my favorite eating establishments, Hudson's Hamburgers. Harley and Howard were friends of my parents, and I had attended Coeur d'Alene High School with Roger, Howard's son.

I was in the middle of eating a pickle and onion (that's how you ordered them), when Howard approached me.

"I hear you are a certified scuba diver?" he asked. "Would you consider being the safety diver for the Diamond Cup this summer?"

I replied immediately. "Yes!"

That summer, a week before the race, I was picked up by Howard and taken to a large work boat. I met the crew and a few volunteers.

We loaded all the diving gear and departed for the site where we would install buoy number one. I would be diving in seventy feet of water and my task was to connect eight, very large buoys to the two-ton anchors (cement slabs) that lay on the bottom. Each buoy's position had been triangulated the previous summer. If all went well, it would not take long to find the anchors and attach the buoys to them. Two dives a day would complete my job. Four days should do it.

That day, and all the days that followed, were all that a diver could want. The sun shone brightly and hot, and the visibility under the water was good. I could see twenty feet in all directions. This was very clear, considering the bottom was extremely muddy.

Our routine was to leave around 10 a.m. and return at 3 p.m. I would use all the air in one tank, surface, take a half-hour break, and dive a second tank.

After completing a day's dive, we would fill the tanks and stow the gear. I would head home, take a shower and head for the Athletic Round Table. It was a private club located beneath the Desert Hotel. The club was the center for all Diamond Cup activities. The Coeur d'Alene Commodores ran the entire week's activities.

I entered the door, descended into the basement, and headed for the pool area. Passing the bar, I walked up another series of stairs that took me outside to a swimming pool. A high fence protected the customers from activities on the main street (Sherman Avenue). Before arriving at the top of the stairs, I could hear the voices of children laughing and playing "Marco Polo," their favorite pool game.

The hydroplane drivers and their wives were enjoying the company of their friends and family. I visited with some of the biggest names in racing including Rex Manchester, Norm Evans, "Wild Bill" Cantrell, Ron Muncey and Mira Slovak.

All went well in the days that followed except for the final dive on the last buoy. On descending I reached the fifty-foot level and began to look for the slab. I spotted it off to my left. I started toward it when I felt the beginning of an ear squeeze. The pressure outside my ear was far greater than the pressure inside my ear. I tried to clear my Eustachian tube by holding my nose and blowing. It didn't help. My ears began to hurt. I knew I should return to the boat, but I was only fifteen feet away. I decided to press on.

As I reached the cement block, everything started to turn black. I couldn't see! Which way to the surface? Was I going to pass out down here? I didn't have a buddy diver. I had to get to the surface quickly. I did remember the words of my dive instructor, "In case of an emergency, hang onto yourself, count slowly, and continue to kick."

Splat! I landed on the muddy bottom. I turned slowly and pushed myself off the bottom, kicking harder. My vision started to clear and I could see the bubble rising. That was a good indicator I was heading up. As I ascended, the pressure eased.

What didn't feel right was the liquid running down the inside of my wetsuit. It was too thick for water and it was warm. Upon reaching the boat and being hoisted aboard, I heard a crewman holler, "He has blood running out of both ears!"

I was rushed to the hospital where I was given cotton to put in my ears and aspirin to ease the pain, which wasn't very severe.

Several days after the race, I returned to western Washington. I was about ninety percent deaf in both ears.

After two weeks, I could hear even less. It was time for action. I began looking for someone to help me, someone who knew what had caused the problem and who could prescribe a suitable remedy.

I was in luck. A physician and diver, newly arrived from Pest, Hungary, was interested in my case. I found his office near the University of Washington. After the examination, I was ordered not to put anything in my ear, especially cotton. He gave me a liquid form of penicillin, which he had developed. I was to put it in my ear twice a day.

On returning two weeks later, I had regained seventy percent of my hearing. By the end of the month, I had regained almost all of my hearing. I still had a little loss.

I thought my diving days were over, but by winter, I was back in the water and having a great time.

The following summer I was back home in Idaho and knocking on Howard's door prior to the races. That year everything went well. I did come up with what I thought was a great idea. I had purchased an underwater movie camera.

"Wouldn't it be great to take pictures of the hydroplanes as they hit the starting line?" I inquired of Howard. Of course I wanted to take the shots from beneath the starting line, not on the surface.

Howard immediately nixed the idea. He said that I was crazy even to come up with such an idea. I talked and pleaded with him.

"Imagine," I said, "seeing the bottoms of the boats as they screamed down the starting line, propeller turning, and water being forced into gigantic rooster tails." No one had ever done this.

Howard said he would contact the Coast Guard and see what they would say. The Commander was not impressed, it was much too dangerous. He didn't want me in the water anywhere near the boats.

Race day came. The boats made their laps, picking up speed. The starter waved his flag. The drivers slammed their throttles to the floor, and monster boats hurtled down the course. It was the final heat, and Miss Exide was challenging Miss Thriftway for the trophy.

A BOOM! Suddenly, a boat exploded and debris flew in every direction. The driver was thrown clear, and Miss Exide sank in minutes. The boats were waved off, and they returned to their assigned docks. The Coast Guard helped the driver, Mira Slovak, into their boat and then the ambulance. He was rushed to the hospital. Mira had serious injuries.

Mira was a hero in the United States and around the world for his exploits. While in Czechoslovakia, he was forced to fly planes for the Russians. One day, he over-powered his co-pilot, descended the plane to fly under the radar and flew to Frankfurt, Germany. His escape with a top Russian fighter plane and his willingness to turn it over to the United States made worldwide news.

While the crash and injuries slowed him down, he was able to return to the thing he loved, racing hydroplanes. In 1966, he won the Gold Cup in Detroit, the British Columbia Cup in Kelowna, Canada, and the Diamond Cup in Coeur d'Alene, Idaho.

What thrills Mira Slovak and the rest of the drivers gave the citizens of this area and the thousands of visitors that came to watch the events.

Eventually the crowds got too large and hostile. Hundreds of off duty police had to be hired. It was getting out of hand and very expensive. My last experience of the Diamond Cup was in the evening, the last day of the race. We were celebrating at the Athletic Round Table's pool area. We could hear the yells and screams outside the enclosure on the street, and we were all contemplating going home. All at once a tear gas canister was thrown into our area. This was not done by the police, but by someone in the unruly mob. We all made a hasty retreat downstairs. Attempting to leave the building, a police officer halted our progress and directed us to stay downstairs. The riot was getting worse. It was well past midnight when the crowds were dispersed and we were able to leave. That was the end of the Diamond Cup races.

Our friend Howard and his wife passed away, followed years later by my classmate, Roger. Roger's sons Todd and Steve ran Hudson's Hamburgers after Roger. I was shocked to learn that Todd passed away while still a young man. Todd gave me the pictures of Miss Exide blowing up.

Hudson's Hamburgers has had many excellent write-ups over the past one hundred years. They deserve to be noted. Not only is the food excellent but the service is friendly and quick. While you are having that pickle and onion order a milk to go with it. They have the coldest milk in town, and the pies are good also. No fries or shakes at Hudson's.

If you have to wait, and there is usually a line, wander into the back and look at all the hydroplane pictures. There is a good one of Miss Exide. When you get a chance to sit down, be sure to say, "Hi," from Jim McCuaig.

The Starting Line of the Last Lap
Miss Exide and Miss Thriftway

The Explosion of Miss Exide

Chapter 12

A Man From Pest

HE WAS NOT just a diver, a teacher or an experimenter. He was my physician when I had the ear squeezes. Arriving in the United States from Pest during the Hungarian Revolution, he found his way to Seattle. He taught at the University of Washington, had a private practice and was a serious diver.

Dr. Spotanski was interested in diving physics and physiology. He was concerned for the health of divers, and how being submerged for any length of time could affect ones heart and brain functions. I was to find myself in the position of being a guinea pig to the doctor one warm, summer's afternoon.

The Washington State Skin Divers' Council joined forces with Dr. Spotanski for his experiments. The participants came from most of the dive clubs in the area. I was representing the Puget Sound Prop Dodgers.

On the day of the experiments, we were herded onto a large boat and motored to a spot just off Aki Point, west of Seattle. The boat was anchored in one hundred feet of water.

With all our gear on, we waited for the doctor to brief us on the dive.

He arrived and told us that we would be wired for brain wave scans (EEGs). We would be blindfolded and taken to different depths. A team of safety divers would be on hand to watch over us. One of the safety divers would hold the recorder, which was brilliantly contained in an old-fashioned pressure cooker. We would be placed in a neutral buoyancy position (neither ascending nor descending). The "lab rats" would then be led into the water, and the safety divers would take them to an unknown depth for an unknown period of time. We noticed that in some cases the divers would be up in ten minutes, and in other case it was more than a half hour.

The unknown is often scarier than the known. It was with some gladness when 4 p.m. came and the experiments were completed. The doctor said he had enough information and was headed for port.

Dr. Spotanski remembered me. That was a nice feeling.

Many of us never had the chance to participate in the experiment, but we still knew, in some way, that we contributed. I've often wondered what the good doctor found out.

Doctor Spotanski returned to Pest at the end of the war.

Chapter 13

~~~~~~

Whatcha doing?

"WHATCHA DOING?" IT seems like such a simple, little question. I'm sure we have all answered it in a smiling, friendly manner. The response I gave one day was not exactly what the operator of the boat was expecting.

We were anchored on a reef on the south side of Lopez Island. It was a beautiful summer day, and we were looking for a good sea urchin harvest. The boat captain, who had asked me the question, had just arrived with a load of people on board and he was headed for nearby Ice Berg Point.

I attempted to wave them off. They waved back and stopped near our diver's flag. I'm afraid I wasn't a very good host, and I'm sure the air around me was a deep shade of blue. I began yelling at them our divers were in danger, and they should get the hell out of there. Seeing a few children on board, my vocabulary did improve. I did yell that they were breaking the law. They said that they did not know and rapidly left the area.

I have shaken my head more than once at either the ignorance of some people or their complete lack of boating knowledge and skill. I have often thought that if people are required to have a license to drive a car or truck, why not one for those driving what could be a lethal weapon on the water.

We had parked the Star at the dock in Friday Harbor, and were going to walk up the hill to get provisions for the boat. As we walked down the dock, we admired the yachts and fishing boats. We spotted a skiff that had been tied to a piling. The owner was probably shopping for food, having a drink or a nice dinner. We hurried on.

We were surprised to see one of the dive boats sitting high and dry on several barrels. We also noticed a large group of captains and divers looking at the boat. We were startled to see a gigantic hole in the side of the boat. The hole was above the waterline so it had not sunk. Drawing nearer we saw another hole in the opposite side.

The dive captain told us his story. He was working the reef on the south side of Orcas Island with one diver. They were harvesting sea urchins. When the incident occurred the diver was working on the bottom.

The captain looked up to see a very large motor-sailor heading their way. A young girl was standing in the bow and there was no one at the wheel. The boat was not changing course and would soon ram them. He raced to the hookah hose, and gave the emergency five yanks. The diver quickly returned to the surface.

The yacht's bowsprit plunged into the side of the dive boat throwing the little girl into the air and back into the steerage area. Four people ran out of the galley with fright in their eyes. They grabbed for the little girl just before the sprit went through one side of the dive boat across the deck and through the opposite side. She was saved by a hair. The diver, seeing what was going to happen, unfastened his hose and swam to the safety of the reef, which was partially out of water.

The dive boat captain contacted the Coast Guard and within a half hour a cutter arrived. The ensign recorded the reason for the accident. The foursome, who had rented the sailboat in Anacortes that morning, had put the boat on automatic compass and thought it would take them safely into Friday Harbor. They had no knowledge that even with the compass working well, the tides and currents would cause them to drift sideways.

No one was hurt, and because the holes in the dive boat were above the waterline, the Coast Guard was able to tow it to the harbor. I don't know for a fact but I'll bet there was a lawsuit that followed. How were these people allowed to rent a half-million dollar sailing yacht with that little education or knowledge? I guess money talked.

We continued to the grocery store and purchased our supplies and stopped at the tavern to have a few drinks. A grocery cart, that we had picked up earlier, we pushed down hill to the docks. It was easier than carrying all those supplies. As we neared our boat, the Star, we again shook our heads. We spotted the skiff we had seen, and there it was hanging by the bow four feet in the air. All the contents had fallen into the bay or were lying on the dock. I assumed that some of the items reached the bottom. The tide had gone out and the little skiff didn't have a chance. If it had been tied to the dock it would have gone up and down with the tide.

Twice in one day, *amazing*!

In the fall, I took my family for a little overnight trip to Sucia Island, north of Orcas. We were tied to the dock. The kids were running around exploring the island, and we were reading and enjoying the sun. I decided to take our little skiff out into deep water and fish for red snapper. I rowed out and dropped anchor.

I had been fishing for about an hour when the fog rolled in. I figured I would fish another thirty minutes and then row back to shore. All at once I heard the roar of a large marine engine and the sound of rapidly moving water. Oh, oh! I hoped the captain had radar. The boat came closer and closer. I was in a no wake zone. I heard the motor slow down, and through the fog, I could see the bow of a fifty-foot yacht. Throwing up a huge wall of water, the captain came alongside me. Holding on, I yelled at him. He yelled back, without apologizing for almost swamping me. "Where am I?" he asked.

I asked him if he had marine charts. He said he didn't but he had some dinner mats with pictures of all the San Juan Islands on them. I pointed out the direction of Sucia Harbor, and cautioned him to go slow. There were a lot of boats anchored in the bay. I rowed back to the dock in time for lunch.

In the late afternoon, the fog faded away. I took a walk on the beach and ran into that boat operator. He never acknowledged my presence and didn't appear to be concerned about operating a boat in reef filled waters.

Commercial fishing is very competitive. It surprised us one day when a Native American, in a gill-net boat, pulled up to our reef net boat and asked two questions. He wondered where he was and where was the Salmon Banks, which were about ten miles south of us. We asked him where he was from. He responded, "South Dakota." I'm still not sure how he got a permit, but we were very kind and directed him north and into Canadian waters.

Throughout my years as a diver, fisherman and boat owner, I am never surprised at what I might encounter, under or above the water. We could all recount many odd and dangerous events caused by boat owners.

"Boat people, whatcha doing?"

Chapter 14

Treasure Diving In Mexico

BURIED TREASURE, SPANISH galleons, rivers in the jungle and unexplored reefs.

This is what my former brother-in-law Jerry had in mind when he invited me to participate in an adventure to San Blas, Mexico.

Having just retired, for the first time, and after several months of inactivity, I was ready to go anywhere and do anything.

Throughout the course of the next few months, Jerry introduced me to "Blackie" Blackstoke (I never knew his first name). A Canadian by birth, Blackie was a longtime friend and treasure hunting partner of Jerry. They had traveled all around the United States looking for gold or anything else that looked promising. Blackie was scheduled to be our chief and only engineer.

Blackie's job, in preparation for the trip, was to build all the equipment we would need to sluice for relics, fossils, chards and gold. He would also work on an underwater metal detector for other underwater searches.

I was to be the master diver. Funny, a one man crew and I had the title of both master and grunt. I was responsible for all the diving equipment including finding a source of air to keep the scuba tanks full.

While I began putting all the gear together, Jerry and Blackie came up with hookah equipment. It looked a little "Mickey Mouse" to me, but if it worked it would be great. I wouldn't have to be lugging around heavy tanks in the tropics. Hookah, named after an oriental tobacco pipe, was widely used by commercial divers.

Air would be pumped down to me through a high pressure hose. A compressor, on the surface, forced air down the hose and into the regulator. The regulator controlled the amount of air I wished to have. Moving quickly made me inhale and exhale faster. No problem with the regulator.

I told Jerry that I wanted to try out the hookah gear before we left the Seattle area. We had planned a camping trip to Lopez Island for the following weekend, and it would be an excellent time to check out the equipment. We would use the dock at Odlin Park.

We arrived on Lopez early in the morning and headed immediately to Odlin Park. We set up the tents and put away all our gear except the hookah.

It didn't take us long to reach the boat dock. Jerry and Blackie placed the compressor on the dock and attached the hose. The hose was about one hundred feet long, not as long as I would have liked, but good enough for shallow areas.

Blackie started the small engine and air came out through the hose like it was supposed to. All looked well. I put the regulator in my mouth. Plenty of air. I gave the guys thumbs up and slid into the water. Landing on the bottom, I headed for deeper water. I reached a depth of fifty feet, which was about the deepest for Odlin Bay. I was about to enjoy my little nature swim when I took an inhalation of air. What a surprise, no air! I blew out what air was left in my lungs and headed for the surface.

Upon reaching the top, I looked around but did not see Blackie and Jerry. I was forced to drag the hose to the shore. I finally spotted the two of them. They were about a block away working in the back of Jerry's pickup truck. I let out a yell! They turned and waved and turned back to their tinkering. I dragged all my gear up on the road, including that hose.

Needless to say, when I got to them, I had quite a bit to say. The compressor engine had stopped. They never left me alone after that. For the rest of that weekend, they worked on the engine and compressor. I hadn't realized it, but exhaust fumes from the gas engine were pretty close to the air intake hole. It was a recipe for carbon monoxide poisoning. They fixed all the problems, and made the compressor and engine safe.

A week later, Jerry and Blackie packed up all the odd assortment of hoses, pipes, diving equipment, tanks and small air compressor, loaned to us by Fred Laister, and placed everything we would need for our trip south into two pickup trucks. They were jam packed.

One truck belonged to Jerry and the other to Al and Virginia Barclay. Al or Albert had recently retired as prosecuting attorney in a small county in western Washington State. Al and Jerry had worked together in the late 50s, and they too had become great friends. Mrs. Barclay came along for the adventure. She had a great sense of humor and was a very flexible member of the party. Behind their truck, they towed a rather large trailer. The trailer would be their home for our entire trip.

While Al's pickup was a three quarter-ton Chevy, Jerry's was a small Ford Ranger. This small Ranger would prove to be interesting for me in the near future.

Having business in the Seattle area prevented me from joining the caravan to Phoenix, Arizona. I would fly down one week later.

The day I arrived we took off for Nogales. Spending the night on the American side, we arose early, had breakfast, and began our plans for crossing the border. As I started to get into the pickup, I noticed that Jerry, a Nero Wolfish-sized man, and Blackie had taken up the entire seat of the little Ranger. Al and Virginia didn't have room for me.

Jerry laughed. "We put some nice blankets in the canopy," he said.

Yah! Thanks a lot, I thought. We're going across the Sonoran Desert and I get blankets. I'm a bit claustrophobic, and looking inside the canopy, I noted I had about a two-foot wide, six-foot long cubicle in which to sit. I checked the door to see if I could open it from the inside. I could. Thank heavens the side windows could also be opened and closed. I could get some air. The desert could, and did, get very hot, even in October. Well! This wasn't exactly what I expected, but we were on our way.

Crossing the border, in 1982, was a fairly uneventful and easy thing to accomplish if you knew the rules, which were simple. Whoever you talked to you just handed him two dollars, more if the person looked as if they had authority.

After crossing the border, we drove twenty miles to the official entry station of the Mexican government. We would need visitor's passes, car and truck permits, insurance, additional licensing and would have our pictures taken. Completing all the requirements, we headed for the trucks.

Before leaving, we noticed two elderly Americans having a very difficult time with a couple of *Federalis* employees. They were going through the couples R.V. and taking everything out. They didn't know the rules. Jerry talked to the Americans and a few minutes later the Mexicans left. The couple had to put everything back in their rig without help. We all pitched in and soon they were on their way.

Our first stop was at a little roadside stand where a variety of foods tempted our palates. I asked about the sanitary conditions of these roadside stands. All the tourist guides said not to buy from them. Jerry said that they were the better places to purchase food. You could see and smell the food before it was prepared, and you watched it being handled and cooked. We all enjoyed our tacos. It was also here that I noticed that Jerry was eating three or four whole jalapenos. I attempted just one, but after one bite, I decided that it was much too hot for me. By the end of the stay, however, I would also be eating jalapenos with most of my meals.

We passed the city of Magdalena. At the Santa Ana junction, we saw our first road sign. Hermosillo was one hundred and seven miles away. This would be our first overnight stop. We stopped at tollbooth number one before entering their freeway system. It was costly, but quicker, and we didn't have to worry about the Mexican *topas*, or better known as speed bumps in every small town that could easily tear out a vehicle's suspension system. We would learn that there were eighteen freeway booths between Nogales and Mazatlan. It would cost anywhere from one hundred dollars for our little Ranger to two hundred and fifty dollars for the big truck and trailer. That was the total cost for all the extra stops.

On arriving in Hermosillo, we headed directly to an R.V. court where Jerry always stopped. He knew the owners on a first name basis, and they were tickled to see him. We parked the vehicles in a locked and guarded compound, found our living quarters and put our clothes and toiletries in the room. We spent a wonderful evening at Jerry's favorite restaurant. My crack about Jerry reminding me of Nero Wolfe was true in so many ways. He liked everyone he met, and he loved good food and wine. He was also exceedingly bright. It seemed like wherever we went the owners, waiters, cooks, all came out to meet him. Years later, I stopped back at the restaurant but it was closed.

After a good night's sleep we were off to Guaymas. It would be a short drive, a couple hours at the most.

Before reaching Guaymas we spotted a road block ahead. The *Federalis* were pulling everyone over. We pulled off the road and stopped. Two men, or should I say one man and one boy, approached our truck. The man went to Jerry's side and the kid came to the back, where I was sitting. I looked up and stared into the barrel of a rifle. The boy, probably a teenager, was not smiling. It was a standoff until the senior officer said it was okay for us to leave. They were looking for guns and I guess they didn't want to go through all the stuff we were hauling.

Seven miles north of Guaymas, we turned west and drove to the charming little town of San Carlos. Jerry wanted to show us this little fishing village before continuing our drive. It was a friendly little town. In later years, Beverly and I contemplated buying property there.

Back on Highway 15, the major north-south highway, we passed Guaymas, shrimp capital of the world, and headed for Mazatlan. We stopped for lunch, for pit stops, and for *cervasa*. We passed through desert country, farm country and mountainous country. It was a fantastic trip. The sitting up and lying down in the back of the Ranger was tedious.

We arrived in Mazatlan very late at night. This turned out to be one of the more interesting places we stayed.

Jerry directed us to a rather large, stuccoed, two-story building with large garages on the first floor. The garage was big enough for both trucks and the trailer. We were escorted through a gate by an armed, and menacing-looking, younger man. He locked the gate behind us, and led us to the front desk on the second floor. While we signed the guest book, Jerry spent a few minutes whispering to an older lady. She nodded and gave Jerry two sets of keys. He thanked her, paid her, took the keys and delivered us to our separate rooms. I noticed a slight look of fear in Virginia's eyes as we walked down the dark and smelly hallway to our doors. The Barclays said, "Goodnight" and went inside their room. Jerry, Blackie, and I went in the second room. What a surprise! We were standing in a beautifully decorated, and very large, apartment. I was surprised that there were three double beds in these quarters. After the long ride, we all collapsed and enjoyed a restful night. Jerry really knew how to live!

Over breakfast the next morning, Jerry told us we had spent the night in an active bordello. We all laughed, including Virginia. She said she couldn't wait to get back home and tell all her friends. I never asked Jerry how he knew about this particular motel.

We ran out of those freeways outside Mazatlan. It was probably more fun now. We went through many small little villages and stopped at some fun little *cantinos*. The beer we drank in Mexico was great.

The village people were a kick. They must not have seen anything like our little caravan. They would walk alongside us, laugh and wave. Quite often, a local policeman would stop us right in the middle of the street, and the children would run out to collect money. Some of the youngsters were all dressed up, and they said the money was for some holiday or celebration. Jerry carried lots of quarters and pencils. He would give each child a quarter and a pencil. They loved the gifts.

Nearing San Blas, our destination, I spotted a kinkajou alongside the road. I yelled at Blackie to stop the truck. I jumped out with camera in hand and crept up on this magnificent creature. As I approached the animal, he stood up and looked at me.

Around his neck was a collar. It wasn't wild at all, just a farmer's pet. I returned to the truck, and we again made our way to the coast.

San Blas was a remarkable town. It was clean and yet still primitive. Our motel was excellent. We were located on the bank of the Limon River. The white stucco buildings, with their bright red roofs, were just what I thought Mexico's cities should look like.

Several blocks away a good dinner was being prepared for us at a combination motel restaurant. Jerry's friends kept popping in all night long. Two men, Jose and Juan, came in with great smiles on their faces and hands extended to Jerry and to all. They were to be our guides, helpers and local historians. After several local beers and a good meal under our belts, we headed for our motel and a good night's sleep.

Climbing into bed, and before turning out the lights, I noticed I had company. A pair of very small lizards raced across the ceiling. I enjoyed them the entire time I was in San Blas and kept food and water for them on the bathroom cabinet.

Bright and early the next morning, we awoke to the very loud chorus of roosters crowning and the music of the Navy band that was stationed a mile away. Before getting dressed, the famous "Bells of San Blas" began ringing. Longfellow wrote a poem about those bells.

On exiting our building, we found Jose and Juan waiting for us. We threw down a roll and a cup of coffee and headed for the trucks. Twenty minutes later we arrived at the beach. Waiting for us was a large, flat bottomed and sturdy boat that would be our transportation. At twenty-five feet long, it would be able to carry all our gear. We boarded and headed for the Limon River. We decided to leave the gear for later and jumped into the boat.

Several hours later we would exit the boat and survey a flat area. We had been traveling through a mangrove swamp with its smell of mold and rotten vegetation. This would not be a good place to get lost in, I thought.

The flat little spot was nothing more than a very small island. Jose and Juan left us and motored back to the sandbar to retrieve our equipment. With our combined weights out of the boat their trip was fairly quick. Thank heavens!

We unloaded everything and began digging and setting up the sluice box. My diving gear would come up with us the next day. We worked until almost dark, and then made the trip back to the ocean.

On the way down the river, I asked Jerry why he thought the area we were working in was worth the effort. Jose jumped into the conversation by saying that in earlier years his relatives had found some very old utensils and tools in this spot.

Back in the motel, Jerry said we would be going to a very interesting bistro that evening. After cleaning up, we left for town. In the heart of the city, several blocks from the cathedrals (there are two), sat our cantina. We enjoyed a good meal. Jerry had saved the best experience for last. He took us into another half of the restaurant. In the middle of the bar was a knee-high, adobe, brick, circular fence. The top was covered in chicken wire. We approached the pit, and looking down saw the largest alligator I had ever seen, and I had seen plenty of them in Florida.

We were told that if any of the customers got out of hand the bartender, a huge Mexican, would pick them up, put them over the pen, and threaten to drop them if they didn't behave. We behaved, drank a few beers, and headed for bed.

The next day, and for many days that followed, we repeated our journey up the murky Limon River. Sometimes I would

dive in the river, and sometimes I worked in the pit that
we had dug. The visibility was nearly zero in the river and
everything was done by feel. I did not like that river.

Upon surfacing one day, I looked up river. About a
hundred yards away, I could see the undulating back of a
reptilian creature. It was coming my way! Remembering the
size of the gator I had recently seen, I scrambled up the bank
and into our boat. I yelled at the group. They reached the
boat just as a large marine iguana wiggled its way down river.
We unanimously decided not to do any more river diving.
While the iguana was not a threat, the cantina alligator had
been caught in this river (although many miles inland from
our site).

That night we ate at McDonald's. This McDonald's was
owned by a Chinese family whose ancestors had come to
this area long before anyone could remember. The food was
excellent even without burgers and fries.

After a week of running up and down the river, and
running our sluice, we finally realized that the spot was not
going to produce anything. We packed up our equipment and
headed for San Blas and our motel.

That night we had a conference, at which Jerry reported
that there was a little island in the middle of the Limon River,
at its mouth. A beacon on top guided the fisherman back to
shore in the dark. It was said that in previous years a bronze
cannon was brought to the surface at this spot.

The next day we headed for the island. Jose parked the
boat off the rocks, and I swam to the island, tipped up, and
started down its steep bank and into its depths. Not again!
I was diving into blackness. I would continue down until I

hit the bottom and, again, started feeling around. Bump! Something bumped my leg. I couldn't see a thing. Bump! "What's going on?" I thought. Twice more the bumps came. It was time for me to get the hell out of there. I told everyone about my encounter. Perhaps they were small eels tasting me or scaring me away.

I started quizzing Jerry over dinner on the Spanish galleons that plied this area and why he thought there might be remains here. He told me in great detail about Manila galleons that traveled the waters between Manila in the Philippines and Acapulco. Most of the ships in the fleet were built in the Philippines, but six were built in Mexico. These eighty to one-hundred-and-fifty-foot ships could carry two thousand tons of cargo and hold one thousand passengers. They carried spices, porcelain, ivory, silk and gems. In good weather, it took four months to make the Pacific crossing.

Pirates roamed the seas, during this time, from the southern tip of the Baja to Acapulco. Escaping from pirates, the ships might have traveled up the Limon to hide. With this information in mind our next adventure would begin.

Several years prior to our visit to San Blas, Jerry had been there visiting friends. One evening, an old farmer told him that as a young man he tied his donkey to the mast of a ship. It was located in the middle of a field several miles away from the river. The mast was higher than the surrounding trees and should be easy to find.

After loading up the two pickup trucks, we headed into the jungle. Bumpy roads, pot holes, and shallow streams slowed us down. We were all happy to be heading for a new site. I still didn't like the experience of being bumped by critters I couldn't see.

We passed Mexican cowboys on their horses and hired hands on their way to the banana fields. The field hands raised their machetes to us. Hope that was a good sign.

Finally we reached the gate of a ranch. I got the dubious honor of opening and holding the gate. I became aware of six or seven large Brahma bulls staring at me. The ranch was a Brahma ranch and this is where we would spend many days. These animals were nothing like the rodeo beasts I had seen in the Northwest. They were neither wild nor mean.

We found an area that was flat, completely devoid of live vegetation, and water filled the spot to a depth of one to two feet. Blackie measured the area. A galleon's length, and this spot was very close to the same length and breadth. There was no mast but since we were here we might as well see what was below ground.

Unloading the equipment, we began the task of seeing what was under the water. We pumped sand and water out of the hole all day long. I would sit or lie in the water, and put the intake hose into the water and sand. The water and sand would exit the hose into our long sluice box. Jose and Juan would look for anything that looked promising and put those materials into a pile. At the end of the day, the items we liked we put in ice chests and took them back to the motel.

I was working a small pond near the middle of our site. Our pump was working smoothly and the sand and water quickly was being diverted out of the hole. After several hours, Jose yelled and we all stopped our work. He said that he was finding pieces of what appeared to be planking. On the sluice other items began to appear, pieces of pottery and some metallic materials. We were thrilled, especially when Jerry announced that the items were not the remains of a dump site.

We continued to dig and dive. The hole and the water became deeper and deeper. We started finding large chards of pottery and rusted chunks of metal. Jerry, Albert, Blackie, Jose, and Juan had carefully filled ice chests with our finds. They kept the fragments under water all the time we were in Mexico.

Albert and Jerry had done their homework and had contacted officials in the federal government. They seemed to be pleased with our advancements. Two weeks into our operation, Jerry and Albert were summoned to Tepic, the capital, to discuss our progress. It was here that Jerry and Albert had to fork over more money. If we did then we could continue our progress. Bribes were all the rage in Mexico in the 1980s. They returned unhappy and nearly out of money. They would have to debate on what to do.

A week later, I was busy underwater with the siphon hose in one hand and my other hand pushing whatever I found into the nozzle opening. Swish! My body was slammed into the bottom. I couldn't move and even with the air hose in my mouth I was having trouble breathing. I was thinking the worst when I felt someone grabbing my legs, or was it two people. I was being dragged backward and out from the huge pile of sand that had caved in on me. My two friends, Jose and Juan, had jumped into the now fairly deep pool and after some digging and dragging they freed me. What a relief! I still owe them. The three of us worked and finally freed the hose from the pile of debris. We stopped for the day, and the beer was on me that night and several nights later.

The next day, on our return to our site, we again realized how lucky we were. I was really thankful. Moving away from the wall that had collapsed, we began digging with shovels. We began to find larger and larger pieces of pottery. Filling all our ice chests, we quit for the day.

That night we had a meeting. Blackie did not want me diving in the pit without shoring it up. We would have to go very deep. This meant we would have to return to the states, rent a large truck, and return with shoring materials.

Jerry agreed but had one more agenda item to discuss with us. The next day we would go fishing, and the following day we would explore the ocean waters and a bay where ancient ships would have loaded cargo.

The fishing trip was great with the exception that I received a nasty sunburn. Jerry and Albert caught two dorados. We enjoyed them that evening with a nice glass of wine.

The one-day dive would be in the warm and clear waters of a rather large harbor. I put on my diving gear, and the boat dropped me into twenty foot deep water. The area was beautiful with no murky water or dirty sand to contend with. I wrapped my arm around a roll of long cable, which was attached to a metal detector. The recording end was located in the boat that followed my bubbles. It did not work well. By the time Blackie heard the beep of metal, and tried to notify me I would be out of the area and in deeper water. We were ill prepared to use this type of equipment. It would have been much better if I would have had the entire metal detector with me. Everyone thought the day was lost with the exception of me. What a nice day for a swim.

Jose told Jerry that night that way out in the harbor was an underwater plateau that might harbor a sunken boat and would we consider diving on it? Jerry agreed that we should go. Our one day trip was to turn into a two day trip. Blackie would stay behind and pack all the gear, and I would dive from the boat without any hindrances of any kind.

The next day, bright and early, we started out into the Pacific. We were going to travel many miles offshore to an underwater mesa. Jose said it was thirty feet below the surface. After several hours of motoring, Jose drifted to a stop and said, "This is the spot." Looking around, it appeared that I was a very long way from the shore. Nervously I asked, "How do you know it is only thirty feet deep here?" They did not have a depth recorder on board. I sure did not want to head down into an area that was hundreds of feet deep.

Jose laughed and took an oar out of the bottom of the boat and thrust it into the water. "Put your ear on the end of the oar," Jose said, "and tell me what you hear." So I did.

"It sounds like something clicking."

"You're right, those are barnacles."

Even without a depth gauge, Jose had to be right. I rolled off the boat and started my dive toward the bottom. When reaching the mesa I checked my wrist depth gauge. Wow! Thirty-three feet it read. Jose was right on the mark.

It was dark, it was cold, and it was spooky. I swam in circles, going farther and farther out with each circle. I was down for about forty minutes when I spotted something that interested me. I swam to the objects, gathered a couple of them and headed for the surface. No sunken boat in that place.

I threw my goody bag into the boat and hoisted myself over the railing and into the back seat. I had found a piece of black coral, which was and is still valuable. I told them that the coral should defray some of the expenses.

That night, over dinner, I told everyone how spooky that place was. Jose and Juan roared. They explained that three years prior the largest white shark ever taken was caught near that spot. "Thanks a lot!" I replied.

The next day, after paying Jose and Juan, and giving our thanks to all our new friends we started north for home. We drove from San Blas, Mexico to Seattle, Washington, U.S.A. In the pickup, besides our gear, were many chests of broken pieces of pottery, chunks of wood and metal objects. The Mexican and American Border Patrol officers were not interested in our "junk."

A year passed before I saw Jerry again. He and Blackie had been living in Kingman, Arizona. They were looking to purchase old gold mine tailings. Jerry told me that he had contacted a couple of professors from the University of Chicago. The married professors were the foremost experts on pottery in the United States. What we had found was 17th century pieces of Chinese porcelain.

Many questions remain unanswered. How had Chinese porcelain ended up in such a remote spot? Had the river changed its course over the years? What would we have found if we could have gone deeper? Were the San Blas McDonald's distant relatives of earlier visitors to the area?

81

Why didn't we return? Jerry was told, before his death, that if we tried to remove any of the Mexican antiquities we would be thrown into a Mexican prison and all of our possessions would be forfeited. That certainly ended my interest in Mexican treasure. I often think, *what might have been?*

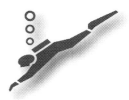

Chapter 15

Reef Netting in the San Juan Islands

LOPEZ ISLAND IS the third largest island in the San Juans, state of Washington. It is the first stop for the ferry boats as they leave Anacortes. The ferry then proceeds to Shaw, Orcas, San Juan and once a day to Sidney, Vancouver Island, Canada.

This island provided me with so many wonderful memories. I had visited the island for many years before purchasing a five acre piece of land near the state park.

Most of the year, farming was the biggest single economic venture on the island. The fishing industry was a close second. With flat, rolling hills and farmland, Lopez became the place to go for bikers. They provided additional revenue for the islanders.

Time and time again, camping and diving became our main reason for venturing to Lopez. When we moved to the island, diving became a source of additional income for us. We also became partners in a reef-net fishing operation. Reef netting was, and is, a replication of the early means of fishing by the coastal Native Americans.

Two forty-foot boats were anchored parallel to each other. Each boat was anchored by separate anchors in the bow, in the stern and by one side of the boat. Between the boats, a net was strung. The portion of the net that crossed at the stern was attached high on the aft side of the boats. Running the length of each boat was attached most of the net. In the bow the net could be lowered deep into the water. Towers were placed in the bows of each boat and manned by at least one fisherman. Lines, off the bows, fanned out and ran down the front anchor lines. Lines were also run from each anchor across to the opposite anchor. Grass reeds were stuck in these lines and they would be lowered into the depths. Salmon coming towards the reeds thought they were running into a reef and headed up and over the lines into our nets. Upon seeing the salmon enter our nets, the fishermen yelled "pull!" The fishermen would pull the front of the net up, trapping the fish inside and between the boats. We would roll the salmon into the fish boat and store them in a large submerged net. A buyer boat would pick them up, still alive, at the end of the day.

Those in the towers wore Polaroid glasses to reduce the glare so they could see down into the water. Speed was of great importance. Our engineer had an electric winch that pulled the net up quickly and all hands started bringing in the net. We had to be ready for the next school of fish.

What does all this have to do with diving? It was those anchor lines that needed tending. If they should part from the cement anchors we could lose thousands of dollars worth of fish. If a storm should blow in we might lose our boats. It was my job to check on the anchor lines and their attachments to the anchors. If the anchor rings were frayed or the marine hardware was rusty, they would have to be replaced.

The shore-side boat was a snap. The side anchor was in twenty feet of water. The stern and bow anchors were both in fifty feet of water. The outside boat (the fish boat) was another issue. The stern anchor lay in seventy feet of water. The side anchor was to be found in one-hundred-and-twenty feet, and the bow anchor in one-hundred-and-sixty feet of water.

I hated going down the outside boat's side and bow anchor lines. It was painfully dark and very, very cold. I needed a diving light and at that depth I could not stay down very long. I remember one dive vividly. I turned on my light and pulled myself down the bow line as fast as I could go. I didn't have to swim and that kept my breathing to a minimum. Down, down into the darkness.

I spotted the cement slab. and made a quick check of the connection between the line and the anchor ring. All was well! I turned my body around and started pulling myself up the line. Noticing my weight belt slipping, I stopped and wrapped by legs around the line. When a diver's wetsuit compresses there is a danger of losing his weights. The diver could shoot to the surface with dire consequences. After a short stop to tighten the belt, I looked around in this gloomy atmosphere. It was then that I saw it! Old, gillnet fishing web was floating in the current and drifting directly at me. Had it been monofilament, I would not have seen it and probably would not be writing about the experience. I released my grip on the line and started for the surface. With panic starting to set in and adrenaline starting to rush I was going to get the hell out of there. Training kicked in, and I slowed my ascent just in time to see yards and yards of net drifting below my flippers.

On reaching the surface, I relayed my encounter with the crew. I still think about that experience. We all cursed the fisherman that cut his nets loose.

While diving on the south side of Lopez, we often came across nets lying on the bottom. There would be all varieties of dead birds and mammals under that evil net. I had to cut my way out of nylon on one occasion. Not fun! Oh, and that is great reason for a diver to carry a very sharp knife. I always carried two. The first was on my weight belt and one on my ankle.

Reef net fishing is a very difficult occupation. Like most kinds of commercial fishing, you spend hours waiting for the fish, often in heavy winds, rain and sleet. One day you might land thousands of fish or more often you could return home, after ten or so hours on the boat, with nothing to show for the effort.

When the fish arrived and we were lucky to fill our nets, it was a big and happy event. Not only would we bring home a large check, but we could fill our deep freeze with salmon.

A buyer ship, from Seattle, would arrive each night to see if we had fish to sell. They particularly liked reef net fish. The fish were alive and not crushed or scales rubbed off. Gill nets and seine nets play havoc with the looks of fish. Our fish got top dollar in a very competitive market.

At the end of each day, we began cleaning the boat, repairing nets, lines and generally getting ready for the next day.

Beverly's son, Clint, visited with us one summer and experienced reef net fishing. He jumped right in and pulled net and helped in spotting the fish. One evening, he asked what he could do to help. Roy, an owner, gave him a bucket and asked if he would like to empty the holding tank of water. Clint grabbed the bucket and began throwing water over the side. After about ten minutes of dumping water, he turned to Roy and asked, "I'm trying to empty the sea, aren't I?

"Yup!"

We all laughed. We made it up to Clint over a few cold ones at the Galley, one of our local hangouts.

Clint wasn't the only person we had draining the fish holding tank. All newbies went through the same routine.

Another fun experience for new helpers was standing in the towers when someone yelled pull. With the nets filling with fish, the towers would lean toward each other in a quick and scary way. They would be dangerously close to the nets and water. Beverly helped me spot for salmon one day. After someone yelled pull, she thought she was about to be launched into the water. I don't remember her going back into the towers.

Our Reef Net Boats with a Passing Ferry Boat

Reef Net Fishing/ West Side of Lopez Island

Chapter 16

~~~~~~~~~~~~~~~~~~~~~~~~~~

The Star

SHE WAS BUILT in 1950 in a naval shipyard, and served the Navy during the Korean War as a landing craft. The portion of the boat that was lowered into the water and let men and supplies off had been removed and a pointed bow replaced it. The area was covered with a pilot house and a place to sleep. A superstructure was built in the midsection and this portion housed the galley and plenty of room for the divers to dress in bad weather.

Beneath the hull, the propeller shaft and propeller were fitted above the outside, bottom of the boat. This tunnel made diving safer. There was less chance to get our hoses tangled. We were able to operate in shallow water and over reefs, without the fear of damaging the blades.

She came with the name Star and to change her name would, according to naval legend, bring bad luck. She was also a star in our eyes.

Our boat, forty feet in length, did have a few drawbacks. She leaked, and no matter how hard we worked at repairing her bottom and sides, she allowed a lot of sea water into the bilge area. We solved the problem in a matter of minutes with more bilge pumps. Being speedy was also not one of her characteristics. Powered by a Cummings diesel, she barely made a speed of nine knots. Our diver, Curt, was a good mechanic and he kept the Star running at that speed. As a result, she was the last boat to unload her cargo of urchins, cucumbers or scallops. We loved her just the same.

The Star could hold thousands of pounds of sea food on her deck without listing to the side. She always sat high in the water.

The stateroom had a nice, but small galley. It was here that Beverly cooked a great breakfast each morning. The favorite food of the divers was her wonderful fried potatoes. High carbohydrates helped the divers fight off the cold water and gave them energy.

The bed in the bow was the size of a double bed and it was very comfortable, even for my long legs. We had a small T.V.-radio combination that worked well even under travel conditions.

Another drawback of the Star was the bathroom. Well, rather the fact that there was no bathroom. When Beverly first found out about it we were out to sea.

"You expect me to not go to the bathroom when we are working twelve hours a day?" she said.

Here again our great knowledge of engineering came into play. First, the crew would not go into the cabin when any person was using the room. We had a bucket large enough to sit on, and a twenty foot rope to attach to the bucket. The occupant used the bucket, went outside and holding the rope, threw the bucket and contents overboard.

Beverly insisted, "I'm not using that thing!" She relented after an eight-hour standoff. It's amazing how natural things become after days, and months, at sea.

We really enjoyed the way the Star responded, both in port and in high seas. I think the Coast Guard liked her as well. They boarded us every time they saw us. It was amusing at first, then irritating and then maddening. Many of the divers in the fleet were a little scruffy looking and some had reputations of using drugs. This was a period in history when there was a zero tolerance policy on having drugs in any vehicle. If a boat had drugs on board and was caught, there was a heavy fine and the boat would be confiscated. Our group was clean and never brought any "stuff" on board. What they did on shore was their business.

We hoped the Coast Guard was just doing their duty and not purposely harassing us. It was unnerving to look around and see a rubber Zodiac with three armed men sitting in her and a Coast Guard Cutter heading for our boat. We would have to and wait to receive the line tossed to us by the crew of the Zodiac. One seaman would sit in their boat, one seaman, with an automatic rifle, would stand in our stern and an officer would read our papers and then search our boat. Since we didn't have anything illegal, they would either give us a warning or leave the vessel.

It was very frustrating to say the least. Time for a dive boat was money. Their procedure would take anywhere from thirty to forty minutes.

The officer once wrote us up for having our Coast Guard numbers too close together. We corrected the problem as soon as we got back to port. We only had one safety violation in all the years we operated the Star. Each life jacket was required to have a light fastened to it with dated batteries. If we fell overboard at night we could be seen from the air. At a cost of just under eighteen dollars, we grumbled but purchased them. We had eight jackets on board. The following year we passed inspection. I was quick to add that we had purchased the life jacket lights, and they were fastened to each jacket. The ensign's reply, "Oh, you don't need them any more on your size boat." Well thanks a lot!

Paranoia was beginning to set in. One year, we were stopped three times. For the divers and captains, every time we got together the Coast Guard was mentioned. All of us were having the same problems, some worse than others.

Before running down the Coast Guard, I do owe it to them to tell every one of the many lives they have saved and how often they have laid down their lives for the people of this nation. We definitely owe them a debt of gratitude. The incidents I will tell you about are perhaps isolated cases, but they did affect our lives.

There were two incidents that occurred in the San Juan Islands that gave us concern. One pleasure boat had run out of fuel and was drifting dangerously close to jagged rocks. The Guard reached them in the nick of time. The passengers had donned life jackets and were awaiting their fate. It was a good thing that they had not taken them off. On towing the pleasure craft, to the Friday Harbor marina, the speed of the cutter was too fast and dragged the little boat beneath the water. All were saved, for the second time, but it was a terrible accident. This first incident occurred when the cutter was stationed in Friday, which was many years ago.

The second incident occurred on a dive boat. The work boat had sprung a pretty bad leak. The captain and divers were safe. The divers were wearing their wetsuits and the captain had put on a life vest.

The water was so high in the boat that the engine stalled. The divers were bailing like crazy as the captain called the Coast Guard. They responded by saying a helicopter was on its way with a large pump that should solve the problem until they got back to the marina. Just as the helicopter reached the boat, the harness broke and the pump hurdled down, through the deck and through the bottom. The boat sank immediately. No lives were lost, but there was sure a lot of comments made between the divers and boat captains. They claimed that all Guardsmen must have come from Kansas, not much water there.

It donned on us one day that what might be attracting the Coast Guard so many times was the fact that we were pumping a large stream of water out of our bilge pumps. Our engineering department quickly solved the problem. We installed a cutoff switch. At our first glimpse of a Cutter, we would throw the switch and the pumps would stop. We prayed if we did get stopped they would not stay long. We would probably sink.

Shortly after the installation of the pump switch, we saw the white bow of a Cutter heading our way. We were working the reefs north of Walden Island. The green urchins were usually plentiful. Using scuba equipment, John had entered the water and sped to the bottom. He returned and yelled, "We hit the mother lode!" Back to the bottom he swam.

Curt was watching as the Cutter was getting nearer and nearer. It was time to turn the bilge pump switch to off.

The cutter stopped fifty yards away. They began deploying their Zodiac. We didn't think they had seen the water surging from the pumps. I walked to the stern and waited. I heard them start their outboard engine and untie the Zodiac from the Cutter. They were going to board us. I yelled at them to stop and pointed to the top of our antenna pole. Our diver's flag could be seen at long distance. They stopped their progress and looked at each other. Even the Coast Guard could not break its own laws. They had to keep at a safe distance. They also did not want to run over one of our divers.

I talked to Curt and told him I wanted him to start work before John surfaced. Both he and John could make their tanks last an hour. Forty-five minutes had passed when Curt stepped off the side. I told Beverly to watch the Cutter and yell if they headed our way. I had to turn the port side bilge pumps on. They were located on the side the Coast Guard could not see. The side next to the reef.

While Beverly watched, I went into the cabin, stripped down and put on my diving gear.

John eventually came to the surface with a stuffed urchin bag. Beverly hooked a line to John's bag and began to haul it in. A crane attached to the side of the boat made the task easy for her. I helped John on board and pointed to the Cutter. That's all that was required. He nodded and exchanged his empty tank for a full one. John then headed for the cabin and poured himself a cup of coffee.

Forty-five minutes later, I leapt into the sea and headed for the bottom with my urchin bag. Wow! There really was a mother lode of the greens. I began filling the bag, eventually forgetting about the Coast Guard. I passed Curt several times before he surfaced with his bag.

I was startled when a hand grabbed my arm. Turning, I saw John. Even with a regulator in his mouth, he managed a smile. We worked together for a short time. When my air was nearly gone, I surfaced. The bag was hoisted aboard and I climbed onto the step and then into the boat. Looking around I did not see the Coast Guard Cutter or the Zodiac.

Beverly told me that the Guard had given up after sitting there for three hours.

When the Star was loaded and divers were out of air, we pulled up the anchor and headed for Friday Harbor. The first order of business, as we headed off the reef, was to take down the diver's flag and then salute the Coast Guard with a cold bottle of beer.

That day we harvested more than two thousand pounds of urchins. We had plenty to celebrate. A most happy day!

The Star

The Star Docked / Lopez Island

Chapter 17

~~~~~~~~~~~~~~~~

Lopez Island

THERE WERE MANY things that drew me to Lopez Island and the surrounding area. There is more marine life in the San Juan and Gulf Islands than almost anywhere on earth. The Japanese current brings warm water to the area, and the many rivers and streams bring nutrients. The current circled around Japan up to Alaska and down the coast. The warm current pushed the cold water in front of it. A dive suit is highly recommended, although my children didn't seem to mind splashing around in the bays. I even knew a couple of high school kids that went skinny dipping in the water.

Lopez Island became the ideal place to dive and we took advantage of it for many years. We purchased five acres near the state park and spent many wonderful days camping and diving.

The south end of Lopez was the best place to dive on the island. There were underwater reefs, kelp beds and all species of plants and animals. On one dive, I reached the bottom and began to circle a large number of rocks. I came face to face with the cutest baby seal. We both stood upright staring at one another, he with those beautiful big eyes. He showed no signs of fear, and he was deeply interested in what I was. I did a somersault. He did a somersault. I rolled over on my back, and he rolled over on his. We played these games until finally he got bored and left. I swam off in the opposite direction. Finding a nice reef, I followed it down to a lower shelf. There, lying on the bottom with a bullet hole in her head was the little seal's mother. She had probably been shot by a fisherman who did not like seals getting into and ruining their nets. They would shoot any seal or sea lion on sight. A cruel world for so many species! I really felt bad for my playmate.

Another different experience of diving, and the Star, occurred on the south end of Lopez. It was a beautiful summer day on Lopez, not a cloud in the sky, no wind, and the temperatures were in the low eighties. Fred was visiting his place and us. Fred, Curt, and I thought it would be a perfect day for a seafood feast. Curt's diving gear was already aboard the Star. Fred and I would enjoy a nice day of cruising.

Off we went through Fisherman's Bay and then south through the Lopez Channel. Passing the southwest tip of Lopez, we headed east towards Iceberg Point. We noticed strange phenomena. The seas had kicked up, and yet there was no wind. The tide was running slowly. There were two foot waves in the open water.

By the time we reached our dive cove, the seas were at four feet. It was nothing to be worried about, or so we thought. We had worked in worse weather. I stopped the Star, and Fred went forward to drop the anchor. I helped Curt get on his gear. A giant step-off and Curt was in the water. He grabbed his goody bag and headed for the bottom. Our boat was rocking in our protected cove but the visibility was still excellent. Very strange! Curt should have good results in picking scallops, I thought.

As was our custom, we always left our radio on (ship to shore). We began to notice an unusual amount of traffic was trying to get in touch with the Coast Guard. It was opening day of the yachting season, but there was more than the usual calls on the air. There were so many calls that the Coast Guard dispatcher began having the boaters switch to different radio frequencies.

Our little protected bay was starting to rock and roll, much more than normal. Coupled with the radio blaring May Days, I ran to the galley, grabbed an iron skillet and a wooden spoon. Back on deck, I thrust the pan into the water and beat it with the spoon. Hearing the noise, Curt came to the surface. While I assisted Curt, in getting back into a rocking boat, Fred headed for the bow. We always left our motor running when a diver was down in case we had to make a quick pick up. Fred hoisted the anchor aboard, which was no easy task. We pulled out of the little cove and ran head first into six-foot waves. The storm was getting steadily worse and strange, still not a cloud in the sky and no wind. Very, very strange.

We headed for home, knowing we would have to pass through the entrance to Lopez Channel. When the tide was running, it was not friendly to boaters. I told Curt to keep his wetsuit on and asked Fred to get us life jackets, which I seriously doubted would help if we capsized.

Rounding Iceberg Point, our fears began to grow. By the time we reached the channel's mouth, we could see nothing but trouble. The strong waves were arriving from the south and heading north. A strong tidal flow was beginning in the north and heading south. When they met all hell was to pay. It was a clash of the Titans. We could not turn around nor veer to either side. We met the conflagration head on.

On reaching the entrance, I told everyone to hang on. I'm sure they were already doing so. I spun the wheel, and the Star roared into a wave so high it went completely over our forty foot boat. The boat shivered and shook. We began to rise slowly. Our deck was awash. Thank heavens for the scuppers that allowed the water to return to the sea.

Looking out the cabin window I could see the reflection of the bottom of our boat between the waves. There was absolutely no water between the bow and the stern. We crashed down into yet another monster wave. The fury of the tide and waves dashed us about. After several more waves tried to sink us, we finally ran into friendlier water. We did notice that our port side was very close to a reef (located in mid channel). If we would have come up from one of those waves twenty feet to our left it would have been all over. The remainder of the trip back to port was uneventful. In Fisherman's Bay, the water was flat. There were no clouds in the sky, and temperature was still wonderfully warm.

We were home safe but in Puget Sound it was a mess. Many boats sank that day and many boats were in need of serious repairs. There was also ample damage to piers, boat houses and the like. Thank heavens no one was killed! It all happened because of a freak storm that occurred hundreds of miles offshore in the Pacific Ocean.

We were very thankful that we all arrived safely back on our Lopez Island.

We lived on Lopez for many years, enjoying a variety of interesting and often odd jobs. We cleaned the bottoms of yachts and replaced propellers that had been damaged by boaters hitting reefs or deadheads (logs with only a small portion of the log exposed above the waterline). We retrieved items that had fallen overboard such as glasses, barbecues and fishing gear. These items were but a small portion of the articles retrieved from the sea floor.

On one occasion, a yachting couple from Friday Harbor stopped at the Islander dock for lunch. Getting off the craft, the lady caught the clasp of her bracelet in the rigging, and down it went into the water. The owner of the bracelet asked me to retrieve it. She said the bracelet was fairly wide with her name, Barbara, set in diamonds. Hanging from the bracelet's side were six tiny chains with a twenty dollar gold pieces attached to each chain. It should be easy to recover. It was only fifteen feet to the bottom.

I searched and searched for the object. The mud swirled around the site making visibility horrible. I rose and told her the condition of the bottom, and that I could not find it.

The lady gave me her phone number. After she and her husband ate at the Islander, they got back on their boat and motored back to Friday Harbor.

Several days later, while hunting for fishing gear, I spotted an object shinning on top of the mud. It was the bracelet! One gold piece was aglow while the rest of the bracelet was buried in mud. I gently picked it up and headed for the surface. After changing clothes, Beverly and I drove to the ferry boat, waited an hour to board and headed for Friday Harbor. On arriving, we phoned the lady and reported finding the bracelet. She hurried to meet us and presented us with a check for seventy-five dollars. We appreciated the money.

While resting from our trip to Friday Harbor, we received a telephone call from a fish buyer. He was working in Mackay Harbor, buying salmon from the local Native Americans. He had a new lad on board and the hand goofed. While unloading sockeye salmon from a gill-net boat, the brailer had become untied, and forty-some fish plunged into the bay. Yes! I would assist the buyer.

The captain was on the shore with his skiff when I arrived. He rowed out to his ship. I entered the water, dove to the bottom with my urchin bag, and began picking up dead salmon. Several large skates were dining on the fish and crabs were beginning to cover some of the others. I chased the critters away (banging them on the head), filled my bag and headed up toward the boat. I repeated this until I had found the majority of the salmon. The captain gave me one hundred dollars, three sockeye and a cap with his company logo on it. I still have the cap. That was really a profitable and fun week.

Most of the diving jobs were somewhat on the boring side. Lying upside down for an hour under a dock or boat was not fun. I cleaned barnacles off docks, floats and boats. Checking buoy anchors isn't exactly what I would call exciting either. The anchors were often in very deep water. It was, however, a source of income. We took almost any job.

One job was not so boring. We received a call from the manager of OPALCO (Orcas Power and Light Company). He had a job for us. The electric company ran a power line underwater from Orcas Island to Shaw Island and from Shaw Island to the north side of Lopez Island. Somewhere between Shaw and Lopez the cable was broken. We accepted with the proviso the power be cut off, and we would not have to work in waters deeper than one hundred feet. Our conditions were accepted.

We motored to the south side of Shaw, entered the water, and began our quest. The first day we found nothing. The second day we knew we were getting close. We dragged a buoy on a long cable behind us as we continued down the cable. Spending less than an hour under the water, we both felt a very strange, tingling sensation. Looking down the cable we could see electricity arching. We backtracked as fast as we could and headed for the surface. Mad as hell, we confronted the manager. He had given the order to have the electricity turned off. The manager was also very mad.

We did return to the bottom and followed the cable to where we could see a break but not feel the effects. We tied the buoy off and returned to our boat. We told the manager his repair crew could hoist the line below the buoy and bring up the cable. The cable was not severed. They then could make the repairs from the surface. Curt and I made a promise never to accept an underwater electricity contract again.

Playing and working in and around Lopez was fun for our family. Our children and stepchildren (Jamie, Ami, Clint and Penny) also loved the island. Beverly had her first salt water dive off Lopez after graduating from a NAUI class. I also enjoyed diving with Jamie and his wife Janet. Jamie was a NAUI graduate while in high school. He retired from the Navy after twenty-two-and-a-half years as a Navy Seal. Penny graduated from Lopez High School and Ami attended there for a short period of time. Clint retired as a Sergeant Major in the Army. He also spent twenty-two-and-a-half years in the service. Lopez was a wonderful place to live. What fond memories we all had.

*Curt Getting Ready to Enter the Water
/ Lopez Island in Background*

Chapter 18

~~~~~~~~~~~~~~~~~~~~~~~

Sea Urchins

"MAKING BIG MONEY in the San Juan Islands" was the lead article in <u>Skin Diver's Magazine.</u> The article pertained to the harvesting of sea cucumbers and sea urchins. These odd looking marine animals would bring in big dollars from the Japanese and South Koreans.

The roe of the urchins, actually the gonads, were selling for seventy-five dollars an ounce in Asia. The five muscles combined with the skins made the sea cucumber just as valuable. We would be paid everywhere from eighty-five cents to one dollar and thirty-five cents per pound for our product.

Reading the article and talking to friends, I decided to take the plunge into this new adventure. I loved diving, and making money was a real bonus.

At the first opportunity, I drove to Olympia, Washington's capitol. I purchased a sea urchin permit and was promised a sea cucumber permit when the season arose. The sea urchin season was a fall-winter fishery and the cucumbers were a spring-summer affair.

George, a friend from Lopez Island, would look into the purchase of a commercial boat. George, a short, rotund man, had an infectious smile, and was excited about joining in the adventure. George was a mechanical genius, able to repair most any type of engine or mechanical object. He would be a part-time skipper and part-time mechanic.

While George hunted for a boat, I began the task of finding two experienced divers. As the fleet swelled in numbers, more and more divers would be put to work. The magazine article was causing a flood of divers from all over the country. Most were inexperienced, thrill seekers. We wanted a reliable twosome who would get along, be steady and experienced workers. We found them in Mike and Curt. Mike had graduated from a prestigious diving school in Seattle and Curt had worked in dangerous places such as below dams. They were perfect.

I ran the boat and was available to dive when Mike and Curt were tired or sick. Beverly was also an important member of the team. She was nicknamed the "gopher." She was the go-to lady. She would "go" after anything we needed. Beverly cleaned the boat, helped the divers with their gear, cleaned cucumbers, helped divers get urchin spines out of their hands and legs, carried tanks up the docks to be filled and she did all the cooking. Not too bad for a teacher with a master's degree.

George's good friend, Dan, was very interested in our plans and wanted a piece of the action. Dan arranged for us to purchase a boat. He would hold the title, and he would deduct a portion of our sales until the boat was paid in full. We also promised to sell only to him. Dan would make sure that the urchins and cukes would be purchased by the Koreans and Japanese. It was a good contract, which we all lived up to.

We took pleasure in picking up our new boat, the Star, in Seattle. We took it to Lopez Island where we would set it up as a dive boat. Our boat, built in 1950, was a Navy landing boat. The original bow dropped down into the water to let people and supplies off. This had been modified to a pointed bow. She looked great to us.

Our daily schedule seldom varied. We left the marina around six in the morning, usually in the dark. We would cruise the boat for two or three hours before reaching a dive site. While cruising, Beverly prepared breakfast in an old iron woodstove. We had friend potatoes, scrambled eggs and sausage. When we worked in fast-moving, cold water we needed carbohydrates.

After breakfast, the crew would mend their nets. These nets were circular with one open end on the top. An iron ring held the top open. It was made of rebar and it was heavy. The bottom of the bag, called a purse, was closed by a rope and could quickly be opened and the contents of the bag dropped into waiting boxes. The bags could hold as much as two hundred and fifty pounds of product.

When we arrived at a dive location, we would put the Star in neutral and one of the divers would dive to the bottom and scout out the area. If the sea urchins were not plentiful the diver returned to the boat, crawled onto the dive step, and we would move to another location. When we finally found a good area, we would anchor the boat and wait until the divers completed their jobs.

Mike and Curt took turns being first. When we saw the divers' bubbles were getting bigger, it meant they were finished and coming up. The next diver would then enter the water. On surfacing, the diver would drag his bag to the side of the boat or we would throw a tow rope to him and pull both the diver and the bag back to the boat. Beverly and I would then attach a snap hook to a strong line that rotated around a davit. We winched the heavy bag out of the water and into our holding area. We continued this process until the divers used all their air, a storm was approaching or it was getting too dark.

We returned to ports where our urchins would be sold, usually at Friday Harbor, Port Townsend, or Anacortes, Washington. While large cranes were unloading our cargo into large boxes, the divers and Beverly packed the empty tanks up to the dive shops where they would be filled for the next day's outing.

Often our customers would lower the price of the urchins. On one occasion, the Koreans wanted to pay us eighty-five cents per pound. Mike and Curt were tired and said they did not want to work for that price and wanted the day off. We all agreed, but after thinking it over, Beverly and I decided that eighty-five cents was better than nothing. We would take the Star out and harvest the urchins ourselves.

While Beverly was inexperienced in handling a boat, I figured that I could get her to a dive spot, step off the boat, and have her motor in big circles where I descended. When I came up I would wave and she would steer the boat close and put it in idle. I then would swim out, climb aboard and bring in the urchins. "The best made plans...."

109

We arrived at a spot where there were too few urchins for three divers but plenty for one. Beverly moved the boat close to shore. I entered the water as she put the boat into neutral. The tide was a little fast so as Beverly pulled away and I headed for the bottom. There, I could hold onto boulders as I inched my way to the urchin beds.

The closer I came to the urchin bed the faster the currents became. I was forced to head back and then up to the surface. On arriving, I found no boat, no Beverly and a tide running. I turned and swam as fast as I could toward the shore. On reaching a small cove, I pulled myself up on the sand and collapsed. I might have also said a few cuss words.

When I finally caught my breath, I stood and looked around. There was Beverly and the boat, only they were more than a mile away. She was doing as she was instructed, going around in big circles. The tide had moved her steadily farther and farther away from me. What a helpless feeling.

I waved and waved. No Beverly! Finally, I saw her move out of the circle and head in my direction. Donning all my equipment and hugging the urchin net with its float bag, I jumped into the sea and swam out to meet her. The water was tearing out to sea. I waved. Beverly waved back or so I thought. Inflating my inner tube I laid on my back. To my dismay, she began making those damn circles again.

I guess she got tired of the circles. Spotting me finally, she motored to where I was floating. She deftly turned the stern to me and put the engine in neutral. I heaved my dead carcass onto the swim step and lay there. Minutes later and with all my gear off, I pulled myself up on deck. I looked at

Beverly and said, "Don't talk to me!" I promptly went to the wheel house, poured myself a drink and headed us for home.

Beverly assumed that my wave was a sign that I was okay. It was quite a while before I talked to her. Before reaching the dock, I realized it wasn't her fault. I should have given better instruction. I apologized.

Mike and Curt thought our adventure was grand fun. No urchins, no money, but we got home safely.

Giant Sea Urchins

Small Green Urchins

Loading Urchins Onto the Star

Beverly Watching Jim
Take Urchins Spines out of His Hands

Unloading Urchin Bags
in Friday Harbor

Chapter 19

Sea Cucumbers

AH, THE SEA cucumber, what an oddity in nature. There are many varieties of these creatures, but the one that spiked our interest had a musical and funny genus-species name of *Sticklepus californium*. Sticklepus was one of those animals that the Asian people loved especially the Japanese and Koreans. The animal's skin was dried for consumption and the five radial muscles inside the creature were used in sushi.

Cucumbers are related to the sea star and the sea urchins. All have at least five linear appendages, such as rays on the sea star or five internal plates on the urchin (the plates encircle the urchin and can easily be seen when the spines are missing). The reddish-orange animal has a multitude of cream colored spikes. They look dangerous but are soft to the touch, a good defense for the cuke. Another unique defense of this two-foot-long denizen is a bit gross. When pestered or attacked the cuke throws up much of his innards. The attacking animal eats them and leaves. Within a short period of time Sticklepus regenerates the missing parts. Interesting, huh?

If people wanted to buy these animals we would be glad to harvest them. The pay was about the same as for urchins and we would be selling to the same people. They had a different season, for collecting, which helped fit them into our time frame.

These animals, unlike the urchins, loved the sandy bottoms and slow moving currents. They were often found in very deep water. Because of the depth we often had to work in a very dark to pitch black environment. With us dragging heavy bags across the bottom, we often could not use a light. The light reflecting off the sand and mud particles made the light blinding. As soon as we ran into the bottom, we swam parallel to shore and with our hands felt for the cucumbers. This was much more interesting than diving for urchins and scallops. Interesting might not be the correct word for it. How about terrifying?

We are, perhaps, all startled at night when, in a dark room, we run into an object. Diving in the dark without the use of light magnifies this feeling. You expect you might run into an outcropping of rocks or some object thrown overboard by a passing boater, but you never expect to touch an object that moves and might be life threatening.

I had descended to a depth that was pitch black. I could not see my depth gauge and I was not carrying a light. The pressure on my body told me I was deep but not too deep.

Pulling myself across the bottom, dragging a heavy cucumber net, I was kept busy feeling in front of me and to both sides. What I didn't expect was to touch the side of a very large shark. Why was he there? Why hadn't he heard me and left the area? He must have heard my bubbles or my vibrations! Maybe, at his size, he didn't care or he was just waiting for his dinner.

Not wanting to be his next meal and with my heart racing I turned my body. I was struck with a very big tail. I headed for the surface. Nothing! He was not following me. I slowed down my kicking. I did not want to get the bends. The water was light enough to see. I stopped and looking behind me I saw nothing that was coming in my direction. At his size and speed, he could have easily overtaken me.

On reaching the boat, I told George about my encounter. I also mentioned that I wanted to dive a long ways away from this spot.

I thought the shark meeting was scary, but I didn't realize that within a month's time I would have a worse experience.

We had motored to the Bremerton Channel and would be using hookah gear. Our air compressor was firmly attached to the stern with high pressure hoses fastened to it. One hose was two hundred feet long and one was two hundred and fifty feet. The hose was clipped to a swivel hook and the hook was attached to my weight belt. For safety reasons, I wore my scuba tank along with a second regulator. If the compressor stopped working then the theory was I would unfasten the hose from the swivel, spit out my mouth piece and put the second regulator in my mouth. The plan was that I either could continue searching for cukes or head for the surface. Sounded good to me!

George stopped the boat and John dropped the anchor to the bottom. George backed the boat up and the anchor was hooked. He then handed me my collection bag. I entered the water and my two buddies started letting hose out as I descended. On reaching the bottom, I checked the anchor. It appeared to be firmly sunk into the sand.

I hadn't been down long, with only a few cukes in the bag, when I noticed the current had picked up speed. Hugging the bottom I started up the sandy hill. I was hoping to find more cucumbers and less current. Strong currents play havoc with your collection bags and your stability as a diver. The currents tend to drag the bag away from you.

I was in seventy feet of water. I looked up! My deepest fear had been realized. The hose, which had been well off to the left of me, was beginning to change directions. It would not be long before the hose would be above my head and then off to my right side. The hose was moving very fast. Our Star had slipped its anchor and was moving very quickly!

I jerked the hose the required five times, which was the signal for "emergency haul me in now!" There was no response from above. Oh! Oh! I dropped my collection bag and began to climb the hose. Halfway up I looked down and saw that my hose was just skirting the bottom. They needed to haul me in! If it became entangled with a large rock I was a goner. No time to pray! I started pulling myself up the hose as fast as I could. The hose was very heavy.

Seeing that I only had one chance left I reached for the swivel hook. I would release myself from the hose and would be rid of any dire consequences. Reaching to unfasten the hose from my weight belt, the swivel hook came into play. With half my hose below me and half above me, and with my weight evenly distributed, I began to spin. At first it was fairly slow and then it started to go faster and faster. I was a human propeller. I could occasionally catch a hold of the hose and then the speed of my spin jerked my body away. There was no way I could shed the hose and use my scuba gear. If I threw up now it would mean curtains. It seemed like hours had passed. I finally noticed that my spinning had slowed and then it came to a complete halt. I was able to catch the hose and steady myself.

I saw a blurry image pass by me. It was the bottom loop of my hose. Someone was pulling it toward the surface. I was soon able to see the stern of the Star. The swim step was inches from my head. John grabbed me by the yoke of the tank and hoisted me onto the step.

George and John helped me into the boat where I sat gasping and retching. I lay on the floor until the dizziness and the ringing in my ears had stopped.

Upon gaining some composure, George told me that after the anchor came loose John raced to the bow and began pulling up the anchor line and anchor. He didn't want that line getting in the way of the hose. While John was pulling up the heavy, fast moving anchor, George rushed to the back to help me. He found the hose wrapped around both the rudder and propeller. If they had tried to turn on the engine the prop would have cut the hose and I would have had been in very deep water with 200 feet of hose wrapped around me. With the anchor on board, and with the aid of a pike pole, George and John were able to free the hose and begin pulling me to the boat.

My anger I had toward them for not answering my call for help left quickly, and to this day I am grateful for their assistance.

I had nightmares for weeks, and as I write this, I find my heart beating faster.

Cucumber diving was not just collecting and selling. The buyers wanted the produce ready for consumption. That meant cleaning the sea cukes so all that remained was the skin and five muscles. Guess who volunteered. Ah, Beverly, she always enlisted to do the worst jobs. But the most messy and ugliest job was to clean our cucumbers.

Curt built a kind of sluice box on the side of our boat. One side extended over the water. It had a hinge on the side board so that it could be dropped down to allow the guts to spill into the sea. Beverly would grab a cuke, there was usually around thirty in the box), and with a box cutter she sliced the cuke open. The skin, along with its attached muscles, was thrown into large barrels. When the box was full, she opened the door and dumped the contents into the bay. The animals below the boat loved it.

One day I made, what I thought, was a delicious looking sandwich. I had baked meatloaf the night before. I decided to add ketchup to the sandwich and give it Beverly. I approached Beverly and offered her the delicacy. Her response, after looking at the gooey mess on her hands and then the sandwich, said, "I'm not eating that!" I guess some people just don't like meatloaf.

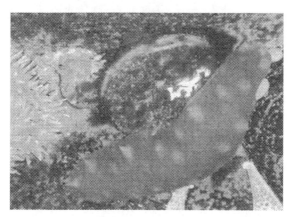

Sticklepus

Our Cucumber Table

*Stepping Off the Stern of the
Star Note the Hose*

Chapter 20

Beauregard

BEAUREGARD WAS A small tan and black cat. Beau, the runt of the litter, was christened by my Texas wife, Beverly. It was the most loving and adaptable animal I have ever shared a home or ship with.

Beau didn't mind the move from Boise, Idaho to Lopez, Washington. He thought living on a boat was about the greatest thing on earth.

He did find out that stepping out on a drifting pile of kelp was not a good move. Down he went! Then, frantically, he jumped on a propeller blade, which spun around and threw him back into the water. I reached down, grabbed him by the scruff of the neck and hoisted him onto to the dock. Off he shot, down the pier, onto the boat and into the cabin. I found him later, hiding in the anchor chain locker.

A cozy cabin, a drying off, and a warm meal and Beauregard was ready for his nap.

Beau learned to navigate the inside and outside of the boat, learned to jump off the vessel, make his way to shore to do his duty, meet visitors and return.

Living on the Islander Lopez dock was not without its possible perils for a cat. Besides the possibility of drowning, we had a female river otter that frequented the docks. She had three babies and if Beau should happen to run into this foursome it could be very bad.

He came up missing one day. I walked all around the Islander Lopez and went up and down the docks calling his name. On the third trip, I heard a voice calling down to me from the top deck of a large yacht.

"Are you looking for a kitty?"

"Yes!" I replied. "Have you seen him?"

"Come aboard," the woman said.

On reaching the top step, I looked around and spotted Beauregard. He was sitting on the lady's lap and being fed smoked salmon. What a life!

Beau fell off the boat several times while we were running. We would stop the Star, grab the salmon net, and haul him aboard. Twice was all it took before he learned it was much more comfortable sleeping and hiding than walking the deck. When I turned the engine on, Beau headed for his favorite spot: the comfortable bed in the bow of the boat.

When we moved to the mainland, I often wondered if he missed his life on board our boat. I did!

Beauregard

Chapter 21

Singing Scallops

ONE OF THE prettiest and most tasty marine mollusks is the scallop. They can be readily obtained in seafood stores and restaurants. All, that is, except for the brightly colored, highly active and musical "singing scallops." Usually identified as pink pectens, the shell's outline is similar to the Shell Oil Company's logo.

The outside edge of the shell displays a colorful mantle and green iridescent eyes. When a starfish, their natural enemy, or man nears these little creatures, they make a little noise and begin slapping their shell together. They shoot up and off the sea's bottom and drift out of harm's way. They can travel many feet.

Years before we started into the commercial diving for these delectable finds, our friends and I would dive for these little creatures. The adductor muscle that holds the two valves of the shell together is perhaps the tastiest delicacy of all seafood. The large scallop cousin doesn't hold a candle to this smaller species.

Learning that we could make money diving for urchins and sea cucumbers, we asked ourselves, "Why not try selling singing scallops." There were no foreign buyers and we did not want to compete with the draggers, who dragged nets across the bottom of the sea, killing millions of other marine life. We decided to canvas the restaurants, hotel and seafood shops on Orcas, San Juan Island and the city of Anacortes. Everywhere we went people wanted our product. With orders to fill we were ready to begin our new business venture.

We often used our boat for scallop diving, but more often we used our Boston Whaler. We were a team of three. I dove, Beverly was the lookout and George tended the engine and piloted the boat. The pectens were found in rather deep water, which did limit my time on the bottom. I would catch many of these scallops above the sea bottom. It was fun diving for the beautiful animals.

It was a warm and cloud-free day when George took Beverly and I out to the reefs located on the south side of Shaw Island. This was an excellent area for "singing scallops." They were plentiful, but eighty feet deep.

Upon arriving at the dive spot, I sat on the gunwale of our skiff, did a back roll into the cove, checked my gear and headed for the bottom. Over the years, I have been stingy in air consumption. I would be able to stay down for a long time. I knew that I would be able to bring up an excellent harvest this day.

On the surface, Beverly and George turned off the engine and were keeping note of my bottom time. George thought I was way past due in surfacing. I should have been up by now. He attempted to start the engine. No go!

In the channel, and headed in our direction, appeared a fifty foot yacht. George began to yell and wave his arms. The yacht altered its course and headed for the whaler. George yelled at the captain that he couldn't start our boat and that I should have been up.

"Would you go down current and look for his bubbles," George pleaded. They would.

I was very proud of myself. The scallop bag was completely full. I wouldn't have to work again that day. I inflated my trusty inner tube and leisurely floated to the surface. Just as I popped my head above water, bam! Something hit me in the head, knocking my face mask down around my neck.

"What the hell!" I nervously asked myself. Looking around, I saw a large motor-sailor.

On board were three people. They had spotted my bubbles and came to my rescue. They threw a large hawser in my direction, which hit me in the head. They asked me if I was okay. I said yes and thanked them for their kindness. I felt like saying that I was okay until they hit me. George had started the little boat and was heading in my direction. The yacht captain brought in his hawser and left for Friday Harbor.

George was soon by my side. Beverly reached over and pulled my scallop bag into the boat. She then gave me a hand while I crawled over the stern and into the boat. George told me the story of the two boats. We returned to Fisherman's Bay.

The state of Washington required that we harvest a sample and send this sample to the University of Washington where they would determine whether or not it was safe to be eaten.

We would dive on Sunday or Monday and take twenty to thirty scallops for examination. We placed the product in containers, iced them down, marked where they came from and rushed the scallops to the ferry boats. The ferry took the product to Anacortes where it was placed on a bus headed for Seattle. In Seattle, the product was delivered to the university. We usually sent samples from more than one location.

On Wednesday, the university would phone us and tell us if the scallops could be sold. If they were too hot in one area it often would be safe in another place. At times it was very frustrating. We would have a large order and not be able to deliver. Red tides were hell on sales. We would phone our customers. They were always appreciative that we did not sell them a bad product.

I believe Beverly enjoyed the scallop industry more than the urchin and cucumber business. We visited all the restaurants in the San Juans and a few on the mainland. Beverly visited with some wonderful and skilled chefs. Being our business agent, she would often trade our product for a weekend stay at a resort or just a nice dinner at one of the excellent restaurants.

On one beautiful June day, we took the ferry boat to Orcas Island. We were delivering scallops to several different businesses. We heard from one customer that a new cafe was soon to be opened on the west side of the island. After delivering to all our customers we found that we had ten pounds of scallops left. We headed for the new cafe. The new owner was young and had an Australian accent. He agreed that he and his girlfriend would walk out to our truck and see the scallops. On the way out, we could tell that he had a bit of an ego. He was telling his girl all about scallops and how delicious they were. On reaching our truck, I opened the bag and the couple marveled at the beauty of the shells. He would purchase the entire bag. He grabbed one of the scallops, opened up a knife and took the scallop out of its shell. Winking at the young lady he plopped the scallop into his mouth and bit down. Beverly and I had a hard time keeping from laughing. The expression on his face was not pleasant. I didn't know if he was going to spit it out or get sick. He did neither. He picked up his scallops and after paying rushed off to his cafe. It was obvious he had never eaten a raw scallop. They are good raw, but they are better steamed and eaten with garlic butter.

We enjoyed selling our scallops to businesses but we liked selling them on the dock at the Islanders Lopez. We enjoyed visiting with people and telling them about our product. We had a business permit from the state and verification we had our products tested.

We heard some funny things when we were engaged in selling scallops. On one occasion, when riding the ferry, a woman approached Beverly and asked, "Aren't you the scallop lady?"

The longer we harvested the better the business became. We had people coming from all over the state. One couple owned a float plane service in Seattle. One afternoon, these very nice people flew up with two friends just to buy scallops. After purchasing five pounds, they turned and headed for the plane. We heard one lady say to her friend, "Aren't these natives quaint?"

Wow! Being married to the "scallop lady" and being "quaint," what more could a person ask for in a wife?

BOTTOMS UP SEAFOOD AND DIVING SERVICES

P.O. Box 115
Lopez Is., Wash. 98261
Phone (206) 468-3535

Jim & Beverly McCuaig
Owners
WA. TAX # 601-282-772

Our Business Card

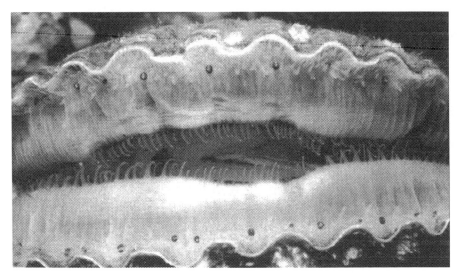

Pink Pectin or Singing Scallop
Note the Small Circles - "Eye" Sensors

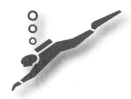

Chapter 22

~~~~~~~~~~~~~~~~~~~~~~~~~~~~~~~~

Jake the Plumber

LIFE WASN'T ALL work in the San Juan Islands. Between buyers not wanting to buy our product and the state of Washington closing harvesting areas, because of ecological reasons, we had plenty of time to play.

A friend of ours, whom we shall call Jake the Plumber, told us to be at the Islander Lopez dock at noon on Saturday. Jake's brother was bringing his purse seiner into Fisherman's Bay for outfitting. He and his crew would soon sail to Alaska where salmon would be harvested. It was to be a three month venture.

The week of their arrival was beautiful. The skies were devoid of clouds and the weather and water were warm.

It was difficult to know when the party started or stopped. Flood lights lit up the bay all night and the sound of laughter, from the dock, was heard all day and night. The natives put up with this for three days without one complaint.

I believe Jake decided he had enough excitement for one day. He climbed into one of his brother's survival suits with a bottle of vodka in one arm and a package of cigarettes stowed away in a zippered pocket. He noiselessly lowered himself over the boat's railing and into the bay. Lying and floating on his back, he smoked a little and drank a little.

Timed passed, and everyone forgot about Jake. The warm survival suit, the vodka, the placid waters and the afternoon sun quietly put Jake to sleep. No one realized the tide had changed to ebb and the water in the bay was silently stealing itself out of the bay.

From his house, at the mouth of the bay, Mr. Fields could see a log floating gently toward the opening of the bay. He left his home, boarded his rowboat, and headed for the log. Mr. Fields would burn the log in the winter, and rescuing the log might protect some boater from hitting it. It was a win-win situation, or so he thought.

As he neared the log he saw it was not a log.

"A body!" Mr. Fields exclaimed.

He started shaking and his heart raced. He rowed as fast as he could toward the beach leaving behind what he thought was corpse. Mr. Fields was in his late 80s, and the rowing to shore, ascending the bank to his house, left him breathless. He managed to phone 911 before lying down to rest.

On reaching the Fields' home, the deputy and the fire department first responders commandeered the rowboat and headed for the body.

Reaching the body, they saw it was Jake. Attaching a line to the survival suit's foot they headed for shore, dragging Jake.

"Poor Jake!" said one of the responders.

The boat was pulled gently over the rocks and onto the shore. The body was dragged several feet. Bump! Bump!

Jake woke with a jerk. "What's happening man?" Jake blurted.

Deputy Dog, a not too enduring name locals gave the law man, yelled at Jake, "I'm putting you under arrest!"

"What for?" demanded Jake.

"For being drunk in public," the deputy replied. The deputy and Jake were not the greatest of friends.

"You can't do that," replied a still groggy Jake. "I wasn't in public until you dragged me to shore! Why don't you just push me back out to sea, and I'll continue my nap?"

Deputy Dog stated, "Go get in the car Jake and I'll take you back to your brother's boat."

"Oh no you won't," said Jake, "that's where the public is."

With the intervention of the firefighters and the E.M.T. crew, it was decided that the fire department would take Jake back to the boat. The deputy warned Jake not to leave the boat or to go back into the water until the seiner was ready to set sail.

Jake was the topic of the Islander's conversations for weeks to come. Jake became a local folk hero in the years that followed. For several years after the event, a "Jake the Plumber Survival Suit Race" was held between the Galley Restaurant and the Islander Lopez. I often wonder if they are still enjoying the race!

Epilog

~~~~~~

AS I COMPLETED this memoir, I was struck by the fact so many scary things happened to me. Then, I realized if you divided the number of bad experiences by 42 years of diving, the figure wasn't so bad. I experienced so many days of fun in, under and near the water. I dove in cold water and warm water and saw many varieties of marine life. The time spent was very worthwhile. Diving in lakes and rivers, the Puget Sound and San Juan, Mexico, the Caribbean, Catalina, and other locations gave me hours of fond memories. The friends I met and the people that helped me and encouraged me were, and are, the greatest! Thank you!

If I were to be asked about diving, I would give the following advice: 1.) Take the very best classes available (NAUI, PADI and YMCA). I'm sure that there are others that are good so check them out. Don't think that by taking a two -day class in some resort that you are a pro, even if the instructor tells you so. Believe me, you are not! 2.) Buy the highest quality equipment. Beware of second hand regulators and BCs. 3.) Plan your dive and dive your plan. 4.) Don't drink the night before or before entering the water. 5.) Don't dive below one hundred feet unless you have advanced training. It is very cold, dark and dangerous. 6.) Always dive with a buddy! And stick with him or her. Keep wet my friends!

Acknowledgements

~~~~~~~~~~~~~~~~~~~~~~~~~~~~~~~~~~~~~

Book Club Members
Julie Pollard, teacher
Angela Chandler
Sally Grant
Jim Shubert
Frank Werner
Summer Williams

Editing:

Miriam Foster
Summer Williams

In Memory
From Beverly

Though Jim is not here with us to see his book
published, I wanted to honor him by completing
this task. It was his hope this book would chronicle
his adventures and love for diving for his family,
specifically his children and grandchildren, as well as
fellow divers, friends and the future generation.

Logging In at the End of the Day
All Good Things Have to End

04164412-00961374

Printed in the United States
By Bookmasters